SECRECY AND POWER IN THE BRITISH STATE

SECRECY AND POWER IN THE BRITISH STATE

A History of the Official Secrets Act

ANN ROGERS

Pluto Press

LONDON • CHICAGO, ILLINOIS

First published 1997 by Pluto Press
345 Archway Road, London N6 5AA
and 1436 West Randolph, Chicago, Illinois 60607, USA

British Library Cataloguing in Publication Data
A catalogue record for this book is available from the British Library

ISBN 0–7453–1093–1 (hbk.)

Library of Congress Cataloging in Publication Data
Rogers, Ann, 1964–
        Secrecy and power in the British state: a history of British
Official Secrets Act, 1911–1989 / Ann Rogers.
            p.   cm.
        Includes bibliographical references.
        ISBN 0–7453–1093–1 (hbk.)
        1. Public records—Law and legislation—Great Britain—History.
2. Official secrets—Great Britain—History. 3. Government
information—Great Britain—History. I. Title
KD3756.R64   1997
342.41'0662—0662dc21   96–53336
                                                                 CIP

Designed, typeset and produced for Pluto Press by
Chase Production Services, Chadlington, OX7 3LN
Printed in Great Britain

CONTENTS

PREFACE

'You're living in China and writing a book about British official secrets?!' The apparent perversity of this undertaking has been pointed out to me many times over the past 18 months, so I should begin by explaining that the book is based upon the empirical research I undertook for my PhD dissertation, *Secretive States: official secrecy in Canada and the United Kingdom* (Lancaster, 1993). For assistance with that project I would like to thank my PhD supervisors, David Travers and Richard Little.

Researching into government secrecy is as difficult as one would suspect. Because it falls under the 'national security' rubric, documentation concerning official secrets cases is subject to the 75-year rule and, at the time I was using the archives, I could not go beyond 1918. I also approached a number of civil servants who invariably refused to say anything on or off the record. One even stipulated that his refusal to comment remain confidential. In the end, the bulk of my data came from reading reports about official secrets cases in *The Times*. I might as well have undertaken my research in China as in the UK.

An ostensible dictatorship is probably the ideal place in which to write about an ostensible democracy. The experience of living in Beijing has forced me to interrogate my relationship with my own society and beliefs daily. The problems that inhere in Western-style democracies seem particularly urgent in this context because we are pressing the Chinese to throw out their system and install ours. Our system, we keep telling them, protects fundamental human rights like freedom of speech. Every time I hear someone say this – which is often – I think of those cowed British civil servants, of animal rights activists who have their mail opened and their movements watched, of minority groups routinely subjected to police harassment, of people blacklisted who don't even know why they are blacklisted; I think of those dusty official secrets files locked up in Chancery Lane and I hope that China – and the UK – can ultimately come up with something better than this.

This book is intended as a sketching of contours rather than a mapping of territory. In trying to move away from conventional narratives about secrecy and democracy, I begin by employing

Foucauldian methodology to crack open existing assumptions about how the state should be viewed. Theorists should be warned that this is not a rigorously worked out Foucauldian reading of the British state. By the same token, the use of terms is sometimes deliberately imprecise: for example, I use citizenry, demos, subjects, polity and population interchangeably to give a sense of the polymorphous nature of the British people and also to suggest how our individual awareness as citizens, subjects, voters or, nowadays, consumers is a product of our changing position in the political culture. In similar vein, terms such as elites, executive and rulers are employed to remind the reader that it is probably futile to try to nail down 'who rules Britain' specifically.

CHAPTER 1

RETHINKING THE BRITISH SECRET STATE

In the interests of the state?

> It has always been in the interests of the State to poison the psycho-logical wells, to encourage cat-calls, to restrict human sympathy. It makes government easier when the people shout Galilean, Papist, Fascist, Communist. Isn't it the story-teller's task to act as the devil's advocate, to elicit sympathy and a measure of understanding for those who lie outside the boundaries of State approval?
>
> Graham Greene[1]

This is an attempt to tell the story of British official secrecy from outside conventional liberal narratives, uncovering how national security policy, and specifically the Official Secrets Act 1911 (OSA), have been used to write the boundaries of state approval. Just as individuals require privacy, states require a degree of secrecy in order to function; the question facing the democratic state is where to draw the line between what information should be kept secret in order to safeguard security and what information should be made freely available to the demos. Countries like Sweden take the position that the demos should be privy to all official information unless there are particularly persuasive reasons for keeping specific information secret. The United States designed a political system with a view to ensuring that information and therefore power was spread throughout different institutions and levels of government by enacting strong protection of freedom of speech. American policy was designed as a corrective to what was considered the excessive secrecy of the British state. In the UK, information policy started from the position that all official information should be kept under the control of the state and only released according to the needs and desires of policy-makers. Britain has earned the dubious accolade of being the most secret of all contemporary Western democracies.

Where does criticism and dissent become unpatriotic, disloyal or even threatening to the nation's safety? While recognising that such definitions are always subjective, most democratic states have attempted to establish legal boundaries that are clear and comprehensible to the population and that resolve difficulties in favour of individual rights. But in the UK, for over a century official secrecy legislation has been a tool that governments have used to create categories of 'loyal subjects' and 'traitors', applying these categories arbitrarily and unpredictably against individuals. The boundaries of 'acceptable' political discourse are shifting and unstable. The British citizen does not simply run up against a boundary that marks off lawful disclosure from unlawful disclosure, a line crossed at one's peril and with the knowledge that the weight of the legal-rational state may fall upon one as a result. Instead, all citizens approach a grey area where it is never clear what activity may be considered threatening to the state. The result has been the engendering of caution and conservatism within a demos uncertain of where its freedoms lie and uncertain of the appropriateness or acceptability of alternative discourses that might challenge the status quo.

There have been numerous attempts to study the effects of official secrecy upon British political life. The inadequacy of previous analyses lies in the tendency to accept the centre's own portrayal of its actions as being comprehensible and legitimate within the parameters of a legal-rational state. This inclination to accept unquestioningly a liberal view of secrecy is a logical consequence of the intrinsic problem of conducting research into a subject shrouded in secrecy. Analysts who try to extrapolate government agendas, policies and attitudes on the basis of the visible tip of the iceberg lack information against which to test their hypotheses.

The Foucauldian approach that informs this study of secrecy avoids this pitfall because it focuses on the effects of power rather than its mechanisms; that is, it attempts to analyse visible manifestations of power as outputs rather than intentions. Foucault argued that an effective analysis of the use of power

> should refrain from posing the labyrinthine and unanswerable question 'who then has power and what has he in mind?' Instead, it is a case of studying power at the point where its intention, if it has one, is completely investigated in its real and effective practice.[2]

Such an approach allows us to step out of the constraints imposed by the liberal orthodoxy entrenched in existing literature about the role of secrecy in the British legal-rational state. This orthodoxy reinforces and legitimises a narrow, unproblematised view of a state that is supposedly constantly reforming and democratising in order to deliver more freedom to its citizens.

The prevailing liberal view of the state suggests that secrecy and democracy are two sides of the same coin. Governments require some things to be confidential while citizens require information about how they are governed in order to make rational choices about the political direction of their society. The debate over official secrecy concentrates on the need to create state structures that can balance the state's genuine secrecy requirements against governments' partisan desires to hide errors and controversial decisions on the one hand and citizens's political rights on the other. Governments 'pour' their policies into the legal-rational 'mould' that policy-makers have arrived at. The task of political analysts becomes one of measuring the effectiveness of these bureaucratic moulds at delivering political goods like 'democracy', 'justice', and 'security'.

Because the secret state is assumed to be governed according to fairly conventional legal-rational principles, it follows that it is amenable to reform in the conventional way. If it fails to deliver justice or security or is judged to be antidemocratic, then steps can be taken to redress these inadequacies. This liberal view, while critical of the present practice of secrecy, is basically content to focus on the issue of access to official information. It posits that with more transparent decision-making, freedom-of-information laws and a generally more open climate, citizens will be better informed and thus democracy will be healthier. More importantly, it posits that change is possible because the British state has been designed to be amenable to reform and improvement.

In practice, genuine democratic reform has not happened. Changes to the secret state – usually defined as the organisations and legislation that are concerned with British national security policy – have singularly failed to alter the relationship between secrecy and democracy in Britain. The reason is simple: reform has been carried out by policy-making elites who continue to make policy in support of their own interests and reflect their own biases. (Indeed, the identification of national interests with government interests has been legally established under the Official Secrets Act.) Policy-makers who write reforms, sometimes supposedly in response to perceived abuses of power, have been adept at closing, rather than opening, the state to wider democratic scrutiny. Legitimising their actions through legal-rational discourse and the demands of national security, they have succeeded in making the majority of the population accept their reforms as constituting positive contributions to British democracy, even if it sometimes seems to be a case of one step forward, two steps back.

By standing outside the liberal view of official secrecy, the extent to which the state has become de-democratised during the past century becomes more apparent. One way to unpack the ideological baggage of the British state is to move away from a superficial examination of legal-rational structures and examine how a piece of national security legislation – the Official Secrets Act – has been used against the demos. The picture that emerges is of a class-divided, politically divided state where voices at the centre dictate the forms of acceptable political discourse. Policy-makers are able to use the state apparatus to control the parameters of political discourse through defining and invoking national security in ways that serve to target and discredit groups and individuals engaged in activities that they consider detrimental to their own interests. Such discourses need not be subversive or revolutionary, nor their exclusion by policy-makers conscious or intentional. The mechanisms of the state have worked subtly to exclude, for example, the voices of women, the lower classes, different racial and ethnic groups and those who advocate causes that fall outside the centre of the political spectrum. The discourses of a white, male, selectively (and often expensively) educated elite are privileged.

According to the legal-rational conception of the state, in Britain political power flows in a linear fashion from the Crown to the people, guided through a network of identifiable institutional arrangements – parliament, the judiciary, the party system, the free press – which ensure that it functions both legally and rationally. In other words, legal-rational structures provide an idealised grid against which to measure the flow of power and provide recourse to abuses of that power. The word 'state', however, has several meanings, and it is worth while to bear its other connotations in mind. In political discourse, 'state' usually stands as a noun, a thing, a bureaucratic entity governed by rules and regulations. But a 'state' is also a condition of being that suggests any given set of circumstances appertaining at any given place and time. Thus the British state is not only a legal-rational entity but also a complex and shifting web of relationships sited within matrices of power that are pluralistic and spatially and temporally transitory. The movement of power, even through a legal-rational system designed to channel it, is unpredictable, its concentrations unstable and diffuse. Foucault tried to capture the essence of power by suggesting that it be analysed as something which circulates ... It is never localised here or there, never in anybody's hands, never appropriated as a commodity or piece of wealth. Power is employed and exercised through a net-like organisation. And not only do individuals circulate between its threads; they are always in the position of simultaneously undergoing and exercising this power.[3]

In this analysis of power it is easier to understand why a weak government can be toppled by bureaucratic scheming or a media campaign, or why a single strong individual like Margaret Thatcher can rewrite the face of politics.

If we look at the outputs of the British state's national security policies over time, not just in terms of the legal-rational state but with a view to how such policies have manifested themselves upon subjects, we can see the extent to which the narrow social base of the policy-making elite has shaped the scope of political discourse tolerated in Britain. Alternative points of view have been quashed. Alternative values have been painted as undesirable at best, subversive and potentially criminal at worst. The OSA record demonstrates this by showing how state secrecy has been manipulated to protect the centre and control the margins according to particular cultural, social and political biases.

Policy-making is not monolithically controlled by the elite but, in the realm of national security in particular, power is highly concentrated at the centre. The word 'centre' is used here to denote the location of policy-making where different and shifting influences, both informal and formal, rational and irrational, can have effect. While political advisors, cabinet ministers, spouses, external agencies, foreign governments and journalists can all affect policy-making without having any formal legal-rational roles, their ability to influence policy-making relies upon access to the centre. Because Britain is governed by a narrow, homogeneous elite of policy-makers who share a class-divided and ideologically biased view of British political life, those who do not participate in these particular discourses are effectively excluded. Individuals and groups beyond the centre have little opportunity to influence policy-making, especially in the realm of national security.

National security is the bastion of the centre's power. By locating control of official information – and, by extension, the writing of political boundaries – within the discourse of national security, policy-makers have effectively cut off the citizenry from any opportunity to engage in a dialogue with government where alternative discourses could be mooted and alternative visions of Britain discussed. 'Threat' definition is frequently based on the interests of the policy-making elites rather than on the wider interests of the demos. At the centre, there is a plurality of competing and often conflicting interests, but such apparent pluralism should not be mistaken for being representative of a full spectrum of views. An obvious example concerns nuclear weapons policy. The three major political parties all advocate Britain's nuclear deterrent. Britons opposed to nuclear weapons – not a wildly radical position – are not effectively represented at the mainstream party level. Furthermore, interest groups advocating nuclear disarmament have been classified as threatening national security. By examining the British state's logic of national security, how threat definition has been manipulated to serve specific ideological purposes and how security laws have been framed to create categories of acceptable political behaviour, we can find ways to rethink the political problematique posed by official secrecy.

Defining national security

'National security' is one of the state's most potent justifications for its actions. After all, what is more important than the continued existence of the state as a political entity? To threaten that security, to be branded a 'traitor', is the most serious crime an individual can commit: in the UK it still carries the death penalty. The problem for all states is that calculations of national security are always political. No 'objective' definition of national security exists; in its place are policy-makers' views at any given time as to what they perceive as threatening. Threat assessment is a subjective art, coloured by the information available (availability itself a product of subjective choice), and by the ideological lenses such information is viewed through. In this way, the political biases of the policy-making centre feed into the formulation of national security policy.

The link between ideology and security policy is relevant both to internal and external security policy. Policy outputs reflect how the state perceives itself in relation to the international system: it might be isolationist, interdependent or liberal-internationalist, for example. Less well understood is the relationship between national security and internal security policy. The serious business of national security is divorced from woolly questions of what constitutes national identity, and yet the potency of national security is such that it undergirds definitions of what constitutes acceptable political discourses within the state. The clearest example of national security concerns influencing internal political freedoms occurred during the McCarthy era, when a small group of politicians successfully articulated a definition of citizenship based on negating a whole range of beliefs as 'unAmerican'.

Such strict binaries make less sense in states that have not made self-conscious attempts to forge a national identity. British identity, having been constructed and then undermined by the processes of colonisation and decolonisation, became especially problematic after the Second World War. Britishness is now too often reduced to Norman Tebbit's cricket tests and irreverent discussion of the monarchy, while the National Front has more or less successfully coopted the Union Jack as its symbol of a particularly noxious kind of Britishness. British identity as expressed through external security policy is dissipated beyond the borders of the state itself. The construction of an indivisible Western security pushed national security considerations outward into a web of interdependent relations with other states, through Nato, the European Union and the United Nations. Even the 'Irish problem' is conveniently detached from the problems of Britishness by physical and mental geographies.

The lack of a concrete concept of Britishness means that identity and threat are subject to redefinition and manipulation according to the whims and needs of the centre that controls national security policy. While threat assessment is subjective, there is no wider sociopolitical yardstick by which to measure threat against what leaders say it is. This has allowed the politically biased and class-biased views of policy-makers to assert themselves through vehicles like the OSA. In a legal-rational state, such biases do not officially exist; civil servants are politically neutral. National security also attracts the maximum amount of secrecy. When governments play their national security card, their position is practically unchallengeable, with the media spiking stories and/or disseminating disinformation if such actions attest to its ultimate patriotism, and civil servants chilled with the fear of being branded disloyal or untrustworthy or of being passed over at promotion time. Even when governments have followed a supposedly liberal trajectory of improvements in political freedom and civil rights, the result has been to impoverish and undermine British democracy by marginalising the experiences and voices of those who do not fall within the 'acceptable' parameters of political discourse.

In the UK, those who use, divulge, receive and/or steal official information are open to the virtually unanswerable charge that their actions have threatened the safety of the British state. In the absence of any clear definition of what actions might be considered threatening, the onus falls on the individual to then prove that this is not so. Whereas most democratic states have sought to tilt the balance in favour of the individual, demanding that the state prove national security has been jeopardised rather than vice versa, the Kafkaesque nature of the British approach is enshrined in secrecy law itself – the OSA is unique in stipulating that the defendant is guilty until proved innocent. The chilling effect engendered by this uncertainty as to what constitutes a crime against the state is also reflected in mechanisms like vetting procedures, surveillance, eavesdropping and mail-opening operations carried out by the security and intelligence services, and informal and formal media censorship. Such mechanisms remind British citizens that they are the potential subjects of the state's gaze and of the state's judgement, encouraging them to police their own behaviour according to the guessed-at desires of the secret state.

The policy-making milieu

At its base, official secrecy policy is about who rules Britain. The structures of the British secret state have been erected in ways that legitimate the sociocultural values of a mainly white, male, middle-class, Oxbridge-educated ruling elite, a group that extends beyond the Cabinet and Whitehall and into the British media and judiciary. Although structures and laws have been established according to the principles of legal-rational governance, these are embedded in and products of a distinctive and not terribly democratic ruling culture. In Britain there remains a dichotomy between rulers and ruled, the assumption being that only the rulers know what is good for the country, and what is bad; in terms of official information, policy-makers alone claim the 'right to know' and therefore the right to disseminate or conceal information concerning the governance of the country.

The interplay between policy-making, political power and its expression in the different institutional frameworks of the British state – the Cabinet, Whitehall, the security and intelligence services and so on – gives rise to national security policies that exhibit identifiable characteristics based on social class and political beliefs. 'Threat' and national security policy are processed at the centre in a closed, secretive policy-making environment. The result has been that beneath the flummery of legal and rational governance, British policy-makers have entrenched a class-divided and politically biased mode of rule which produces policies that fail both to represent the British polity as a whole and to provide a genuine 'national security' designed to protect the rights and interests of all citizens. While differences of opinion can be detected, overall the policy-making elite has expressed particular ideological biases. The elite resembles traditional models of a ruling class in the sense that it is overtly capitalist, white and sited to the right of the political spectrum. In its hands, national security policy becomes an instrument by which political dissent can be cut off, and leftwing alternatives discredited. Security policy has been biased not only against the ruled but also against the left. In essence, political views antipathetic to the elites have been criminalised.

Such political and class biases have had concrete negative consequences for British national security and for democracy. By protecting itself according to Old Boys' rules, the centre has allowed national security to be jeopardised, most glaringly when narrow, Oxbridge-biased recruitment policies were so successfully exploited by Soviet intelligence. Democracy has been jeopardised through the disenfranchisement of a range of views that might contribute to rather than undermine the development of the British state.

The ruling establishment does not simply 'make' policy; it also writes the legal-rational state in which policy-making occurs. Thus security policy is formulated within a politically biased milieu in which national security, loyalty and threat are defined according to the ideological biases of a privileged group rather than according to more neutral or objective assessments. Membership in the elite means that the rules of the legal-rational state are supplanted by other rules that derive from shared cultural and social positions. The British elite has consistently refused to believe in the possibility of its own disloyalty to the British state; only the ruled are capable of disloyalty. Furthermore, the elite has signalled that it is above the law it makes, assuming one set of rules for itself and one for those it rules. Thus the illegal behaviour of the security and intelligence services has been sanctioned because national security issues are considered so important that the centre allows specific groups to operate outside the boundaries of the legal-rational state.

The OSA offers a way into the policy-making milieu by

providing a specific national security output which can be analysed. In contrast to the contingency planning of the armed forces, the policies and scenarios of which might never be tested, internal security policies target individuals directly. There is a direct correlation between threat and policy, although this correlation does not always hold true at the legal-rational level. Threats may be designated in theory but, in practice, steps are not always taken to alleviate them. Both rightwing and leftwing extremism have been defined as threatening to state stability, but rightwing activities have been largely ignored by the state. By examining what steps have been taken – looking through a Foucauldian lens at the practice of policy rather than simply at its intentions – we can begin to extrapolate what the state not only formally defines as threatening but also in practice reacts to as threatening, thus producing a more accurate picture of its national security concerns.

The first clear image that emerges is the dichotomy between the power at the policy-making centre and the lack of political efficacy at the margins. National security policy is in the hands of those who have infinite belief in their own loyalty and endless suspicions about everyone else; there is a clear us/them binary, with the loyalty of those 'inside' the policy-making apparatus as virtually beyond question. There is no clearly defined border between inside and outside; the policy-making centre can encompass interest groups or newspaper editors as well as prime ministers, as one would expect given the mercurial flow of political power. However, decision-making remains a closed process because there is no structured way in which groups and individuals can achieve influence. Decisions are made subjectively by those within and traditionally these decisions have not been challengeable. Governments need only utter the words 'national security' and the door to democratic participation is firmly shut.

The second image is of a policy-making elite that shares a rightwing political bias, although this is often latent rather than overt. An exegesis of decades of OSA cases provides the outlines of this bias and its consequences upon the British state. Such findings allow us first to posit the existence of a divided society where, as far as national security goes, power remains concentrated in the hands of the rulers over the ruled. Second, they allow us to identify the notoriously nebulous political biases of the 'ruling class'.

There is a plurality of views within the corridors of power: Buddhists, Quakers and Soviet spies coexist within the ranks of the quintessentially Oxbridge Old Boys elite. This plurality and the dispersal of power it represents erupts at different nodes and in different guises. A multiplicity of views was especially visible during the Thatcher era, when the battle between conflicting interests at the centre erupted in the courts and the media. But a plurality of views at the policy-making centre does not diminish the fact that the policy that eventually emerges exhibits the clear biases of a narrow elite that tends to be white, male and educationally privileged. It would not necessarily matter if everyone in power graduated from Oxbridge if this had no consequences for the operation of democracy in Britain, but it does. The prevailing political norms are expressed in policy which in its effects sanctions certain values and interests that the state wishes to sustain at the expense of others that it perhaps wishes might go away.

The media have played an important part in constructing the approach to official secrecy. The role of the media has been to campaign for reform, demanding greater openness and freedom of information, a task that seems to set them in opposition to the policy-making centre. If one questions this liberal orthodoxy, however, one finds that the real role of the media has been to amplify the centre's views of acceptable political discourse. The media's representation of official secrecy does not reflect their practice. Instead, they articulate and reinforce views of secrecy that are framed almost entirely by the debate over the use and abuse of power at the centre and that advocate legal-rational reform. The margins are once again reduced to the function of audience, cheering the hero and booing the villain, the ideological lines firmly drawn around an elite-defined version of acceptable political discourse. The demos-as-audience receives its information filtered through a mainstream media, which, despite its posturing, is located at the centre and constructs its world view accordingly.

While the media are among the most voracious critics of official secrecy, they are seldom themselves its victims. The media support rather than 'report' the centre's view by publicising only those cases that buttress the prevailing orthodoxy of the liberal democratic state. The debate over who has access to official information is therefore constructed along legal-rational lines, where particular cases are sensationalised in order to support the centre's view of the state. The everyday, ordinary person's experience of official secrecy is excluded.

Rulers and ruled are thus divided by the centre's narrow view of acceptable political boundaries. Official secrets cases invariably reflect the centre's idea of the acceptable norm. Down through the decades, Bolsheviks and antinuclear campaigners have been deemed threatening, while fascists and Oxbridge graduates have been treated indulgently for similar offences. Trade unionism has been banned from Government Communications Headquarters (GCHQ) to protect national security while, in the wake of horrendous security failures, MI5 has been asked to reform itself. Sarah Tisdall, a junior Foreign Office clerk, was sent to prison for unauthorised disclosure while Clive Ponting, a senior mandarin, was acquitted months later for a similar offence. It is always the loyalty at the margins that is questioned. Policy-makers, in drawing their definitions, exclude themselves. Those on the left of the political spectrum are attacked rather than those on the right. The way the OSA has been applied makes this dualism obvious. If the central issue of official secrecy is who rules, then the answer lies in political representation: whoever is represented in the security policy-making process participates in the writing of the boundaries of acceptable political discourse.

CHAPTER 2

THE BUREAUCRATISATION OF SECRECY

Pre-twentieth-century secrecy

The invention of a state disciplinary apparatus designed to collect, collate and control official information was remarkably rapid. From the informality of information control during the Victorian era, by 1912 the state had established an institutional regime of control, including the parliamentary lobby system, the security and intelligence services, strict official secrecy laws and a registry of aliens. There was no comprehensive 'master plan' to erect laws and institutions designed to entrench a division between rulers and ruled. The new regime emerged from a fortuitous dovetailing of national security concerns and political-bureaucratic interests as the policy-making centre took measures to shore up its control over information, which was slipping in the face of increasing democratisation. Paradoxically, it was the arrival of democracy that spawned a concomitant movement to close the policy-making process to democratic influence.

The agenda behind the flurry of national security legislation around the turn of the century was supposedly the looming German threat which compelled the British state to take measures to prepare itself for possible confrontation. The 1911 Official Secrets Act was passed during the Agadir Crisis, with German gunboats threatening British spheres of influence and Lloyd George warning of impending war. In such an atmosphere, parliament, the press and the public acquiesced to legislation that had been previously opposed. Such measures signalled the move from the increasingly ineffective, informal, *de facto* practice of administrative secrecy to the invention of official secrecy as a bureaucratic and legal category within the British state. The state legitimated the changes by invoking the national security threat. But while Germany provided a convincing public rationale for the move to 'official' secrecy and surveillance, the real reason lay in the assault that democratisation was inflicting on the ruling classes' traditional hold over the state.

The enlargement of the electoral franchise and of the state

apparatus itself, and the rise of the commercial press, all contributed to the invention of the secret state. As though to mitigate the
possible effects of increasing power and knowledge among its
demos, policy-makers moved to curb and control the dissemination
of official information. Before the mid-nineteenth century, secrecy
was the accepted style of rule: during the Victorian era, self-conscious attempts had to be made to justify secrecy to the people – and
to acquire their complicity in such measures.

It is imprecise to term what historically went on inside the
British state 'secrecy', as if a conscious decision to be secretive
rather than open had been taken. Secrecy is rooted in the historical circumstances that gave rise to the British state and particularly in the idea that there existed a natural ruling class. This
class – originally headed by a sovereign approved by no less a
personage than God – saw itself as the natural heirs to the leader-
ship of Britain and as such it was accepted by the political
community. Although the composition of the ruling class grew
more mixed as the centuries progressed, it remained a preserve of
the well born, with the newly wealthy reluctantly being granted
an entrée. The ruling class was a tightknit social group. Its
members not only governed together, but went to the same
schools, the same dinner parties and even married the same sort
of girl (since they were and remain almost invariably male). They
saw the world the same way and accepted their vision as the
correct vision by which to guide the ship of state. Secrecy as a
part of this rule was as natural as breathing. Decision-making
took place in private. It would not have occurred to policy-
makers to volunteer information about decision-making, nor to
the demos to demand it; in the extant political order, rulers ruled
and subjects obeyed.

This traditional acceptance of ruling-class primacy was eroded
as political, economic and social change altered the British political landscape. The construction of a political system based on
rule by consent by at least some of the people rather than whim
of the sovereign has been the goal of reformers from Magna Carta
on; some eight centuries later, universal suffrage had nearly
arrived. Despite such advances in the democratic process, the
idea of a 'natural' ruling class persisted; now it was overlaid with
the legitimating framework of the legal-rational state. Victorian
moral certitudes that had enabled government to function along
consensual, *de facto* lines were undermined by modernisation and
replaced with legal-rational practices that gave the policy-making
process a patina of legitimacy. What had been 'moral' became

'legal-rational'. The transformation was theoretically a progressive move by a modernising state keen to shed the arbitrary exercise of sovereign power and replace it with the legitimate and rational use of democratic power. But this legitimacy was sleight of hand; at its heart, national security policy-making became more, not less, arbitrary as policy-makers placed legal barriers between themselves and the citizenry. In important respects the state became less democratic because of the concentration of power over national security policy and its effects on political freedoms.

Secrecy, once a by-product of oligarchic rule, now became a deliberate instrument of political power. In the hands of British policy-makers, national security proved to be a concept that enabled them to bridge the gap between government control of information as a matter of practice to such control as a matter of right. What constituted 'threat' had always involved calculations based upon prejudices and antipathies towards external actors, shored up by appeals to national morals. The difference now lay in that, between 1889 and 1912, the process of threat definition became institutionalised under a panoply of new laws, practices and organisational changes that excluded the demos.

Legal-rational structures were bestowed upon the hermetic decision-making process, beginning in 1889 when the government entrenched its rights over official information in the first Official Secrets Act. With this law, ignorance and knowledge were placed into legally defined categories. The foundations thus were laid for a state apparatus that codified the division between ruler and ruled in the face of contrary trends towards democratisation and pluralism. The exigencies of national security, claimed the centre, demanded that the citizen be condemned to ignorance, not because he or she was a member of the subject class, but because the state required excessive secrecy in order to remain secure.

This shift to an institutional regime of information control had a massive impact upon the evolution of modern political freedoms. With the advent of ideologies, democratisation and revolution, challenges to the status quo increasingly emanated from within the state itself. Legitimate political challenges were ruled out of British political discourse through the new disciplinary regime enacted by this institutionalisation. Throughout the body politic, categories of deviance – here in the form of the binary of loyalty/threat – were established. Because an actual definition of what constituted loyal or threatening discourse did not exist, the power to formulate arbitrary definitions according to political whim became the prerogative of the state. National security was what policy-makers said it was. They were not required to offer any explanation or information about their decisions. Since the process was now entrenched in law, the demos was assured that the processes by which national security was fixed ran along the twentieth-century tracks of rational government. But national security policy-making was cloaked in secrecy, thereby removing the entire debate about Britain's political direction and national survival from any possibility of democratic participation. National security hinged only upon the rulers' reassurance to the populace: 'trust us'.

Uncertainty about where the boundary between loyalty and threat lay engendered increasing conservatism in the political community. The citizen's judgement was severely curtailed. Who knew what the Germans were up to? What seemingly innocent move might assist them in their imminent invasion? Lacking access to information, citizens had no choice but to follow the dictates of the political centre. Because policy-makers alone had access to information, they alone could claim to see the national security picture; they alone could arbitrate. Pressing its advantage, the centre pushed out the boundaries of its definition of threat, marginalising whole tracts of political discourse on the grounds that they jeopardised national security. A citizenry consigned to ignorance could never mount an effective challenge to policy-making constructed in such conditions.

The erosion of the effectiveness of informal secrecy through the nineteenth century led to the setting up of a new regime to control the flow of official information. This regime, although it purported to follow the legitimising trajectory of a modernising legal-rational state, had no intention of operating along objective definitions of threat or on 'rational' assessments of national security. The laws enacted had little to do with the requirements of a modern state and everything to do with reasserting slipping official control over information – the great source of its power – in the face of increasing democratisation.

The origins of the modern secret state

The apparently overnight sensation of the secret state had been stealthily evolving throughout the nineteenth century. Within the Victorian administrative culture, reliability and discretion had been secured through appeals to moral probity, appeals made resonant through the homogeneous make-up and culture of the civil servants themselves. The shared values of the ruling culture were adhered to and perpetuated within a civil service largely populated by members of the elite. As the bureaucracy expanded, necessitating the recruitment of those outside the elite's immediate purview, this shared culture of discretion was harder to maintain. Appealing to the patriotic need to protect national security proved to be a potent way of coopting new public servants into the administrative culture of secrecy; when this 'carrot' did not work, the 'stick' of legal action was applied.

The Official Secrets Acts of both 1889 and 1911 were culminations of particular concerns within the state over unauthorised disclosure, although the legislation in both cases was presented to parliament as urgent solutions designed to meet external threats. Throughout the nineteenth century, the ethos of governmental discretion was being eroded as official information became a valuable commodity; its growth in commercial and political value led to increasing incidence of unauthorised disclosure. Governments struggled to prevent the increasing incidence of privately held official documents and letters finding their way into the marketplace and, as the material being disclosed grew more current and more sensitive to governments in power, the need to curtail leaks became more acute.

Unauthorised disclosure had long been regarded seriously but the offence was considered a moral rather than a legal one. In 1873 the Permanent Undersecretary of the Treasury described leaking as 'the worst fault a civil servant can commit. It is on the same footing as cowardice by a soldier.'[1] As the state apparatus grew in size, individuals within the public sector proved to be increasingly unreliable and reporters looking for scoops created a ready market for their material. The leaks process directly challenged the state's traditional monopoly on information provision.

Existing methods of dealing with the problem were somewhat hit and miss. In 1833 the Foreign Office successfully prevented the sale of eighteenth-century documents concerning foreign relations, but failed four years later in its attempts to prevent publication of Marquess Wellesley's 1809 correspondence from Spain. The Foreign Office failed again in 1847 when *The Times*, claiming it was in the public interest, published Viscount Castlereagh's correspondence about the 1815 Vienna Conference. While such revelations were embarrassing, the information published was of historical rather than contemporary relevance. As the century progressed, disclosures began to have more direct relevance to government activities as civil servants began leaking current information to newspapers.

The government was keen to staunch the flow of illicit disclosures but found existing legislation ineffective. In 1878 the government failed to gain a conviction against a disenchanted temporary Foreign Office clerk, Charles Marvin, who had vowed 'to place upon the market every piece of information that chance threw in my way'.[2] Marvin sold the text of an Anglo–Russian agreement prepared for the Congress of Berlin – intended to be read in the House and published in *The Times* – to a rival newspaper. When the government traced Marvin as the source of the leak, they had to charge him with the theft of government paper, upon which he allegedly copied out the terms of the agreement. Marvin had used his own paper and the magistrate dismissed the case.

Such failures suggested that the *de facto* strategies of control needed to be buttressed by legal coercion. Crown servants who divulge official information without express authorisation may, by such acts, jeopardise national security or misuse information for corrupt and criminal purposes or simply act carelessly – acts that the criminal law can 'rationally' deal with. But, more nebulously, civil servants can cause harm breaking the cardinal rule of 'discretion' and it is this violation of trust that is seen as damaging, not just to isolated administrative departments, individuals or governing parties but to the British state *per se*. One way of reading the legal conflation of espionage with unauthorised disclosure is as a measure of the seriousness with which violations of official trust were regarded. In its early stages the OSA was known as the Breach of Official Trust Bill, thereby neatly combining in its title both legal-rational and moral concerns. The change to the word 'secrets' in the title signalled the preeminence of national security, a more 'rational' and therefore politically expedient justification than supplications to mandarin ethicality suggested by the word 'trust'. This overtly political purpose was cloaked by invoking 'national security' as the primary justification for the OSA, a compelling public rationale.

Just how important was national security to the state's construction of the new secrecy regime? Victorian legislators did not regard espionage as an overly serious problem.[3] Intelligence activities were at something of a nadir in the late nineteenth century, with spying considered an unfit occupation for gentlemen. The Duke of Wellington reputedly picked up his intelligence on colonial conflicts from the newspapers; domestic political surveillance was similarly unsophisticated. When the Home Office undertook an examination into the activities of refugees from the Paris Commune in 1871, it wrote to Karl Marx, who obligingly provided an account of the activities of the Workingmen's International. The government had provided an intelligence budget of £100,000 a year during the Napoleonic Wars, but by the 1880s this had dropped to £23,000. Operations abroad tended to involve colonial intriguing where bribery and espionage were more effective and less likely to offend moral sensibilities. Until 1900, what concerns there were involved France and Russia, which were thought to operate spy networks.

There were, of course, espionage threats. For foreign powers, the civil service was the obvious source of information. In 1887 a dockyard draughtsman sold warship plans to an unspecified country, probably France. He was dismissed for breach of confidence, but could not be prosecuted due to lack of evidence. It was this affair that spurred the Admiralty to draft a proposal for what would eventually become the Official Secrets Act 1889. Although espionage provided the immediate impetus for legislation, from the first draft of the Admiralty's 1889 bill it was apparent that the proposed law was intended to provide legislation to cover both espionage and leaks. In his introduction to the bill, the Lord Chancellor indicated as much:

> If any person so communicates to another country adversely to the interests of this country, it is made felony and the subject of a severe penalty. ... Another class of offenses is the disclosure of official secrets. When a person who is holding, or has held, office under Her Majesty, or has in his possession or control any official document, should in like manner communicate with those who become the Queen's enemies severe penalties are enacted.[4]

From the outset the law was intended to catch less grave offences such as the communication of information to newspapers. There were fears that the ambit of the bill was too extensive. In the debate that ensued, Lord Herschel told the House that 'although I entirely approve of the general objects of the Bill, I cannot help thinking that in some of its details it goes too far'. Purporting to deal with spies, the OSA 1889 also targeted civil servants. The guidelines for release of official information were straightforward: all official information was covered, and no civil servant had the right to disclose it without authorisation.

Despite the wide purview of the 1889 Act, its limitations in dealing with both espionage and leaks cases were soon obvious. The burden of proof – as is usual – fell upon the prosecution, but this made convictions difficult to obtain in espionage cases.

Sentences were relatively light and the threat of prosecution failed to stop civil servants from leaking. One of its most serious failings was the extent of its reach: the 1889 OSA applied only to Crown servants and some government contractors and, although all kinds of official information were covered, it was an offence only if the recipient of the information was found to violate the interests of the state or the public interest.[5] The Act did not attack the press, which provided so many inducements for civil service disclosure, nor did it curtail the flow of high quality military information that was finding its way into newspapers. In March 1908 a newspaper article horrified both the War Office and the Admiralty when it described in detail Dover Harbour's modern defences. Such concerns were certainly justified: the Germans found it 'easier, likely to be more accurate, less dangerous and certainly cheaper, for a German agent to get information by reading newspapers'.[6] The law did not allow for the arrest or investigation of suspected spies; it did not even make passing military secrets in peacetime an offence. An ex-Army draughtsman caught selling military secrets to the French had to be charged under the breach of confidence law, which carried a maximum sentence of twelve months, even though his actions clearly threatened national security.

Yet the same Act was already being stretched beyond its ostensible national security designs. An employee in the supply reserve depot with access to details of government supply contracts offered information to a government contractor concerning the prices charged by rival firms. In court the defence pointed out that the defendant did not know the information was confidential, nor was he familiar with the Official Secrets Act. The employee was found guilty, although the punishment prescribed was that he be bound over, a leniency that would soon disappear.

As such limitations became apparent, attempts were made to tighten the legislation. The Admiralty and the War Office had been discussing the need to strengthen espionage laws, step up political surveillance, and place restrictions on aliens since 1906, while the Committee of Imperial Defence (CID), which wanted to prohibit unauthorised disclosure completely, began to draft appropriate legislation in 1904. A 1908 attempt to enact some changes was thwarted by media protest. The government realised the political climate was not yet ripe for the introduction of greater national security powers.

While it was the powers to curb unauthorised disclosure that the government sought to shore up, it was the German threat that in the end provided the excuse it needed to take decisive action. The government was sanguine about the German espionage threat: in 1909 its German counterespionage head Colonel James Edmonds commanded a budget of £200 and two assistants. The German threat was in fact muted: while German naval intelligence had been reconnoitring landing places, the location of naval bases and so on since 1902, as late as 1914 there was no organised spying operation in Britain. According to German 1899 defence estimates, the British navy was superior; plans to invade Britain were considered and discarded again in 1907.

The electorate, unlike the government, was restive. Fuelled by press reports and best-selling novels predicting an impending German invasion, the British public was transformed into a nation of would-be spy-catchers who were constantly reporting sightseeing continental tourists and 'suspicious' foreigners to the authorities. The contribution of fiction writers to the origins of modern British intelligence is emphasised in histories of the secret service: William Le Queux's novels were particularly influential. His best-selling *Spies of the Kaiser: plotting the downfall of England* described in detail a German invasion. It was originally serialised in a newspaper in 1906 which held a 'Have You Seen a Spy?' competition – prize, ten pounds. The resulting readers' correspondence found its way into the files of Edmonds who, with his minuscule budget and manpower contingent, sought to convince his superiors of the seriousness of the threat posed by a German fifth column of waiters, barbers and hotel employees who would rise up to aid the eventual invasion. The CID subcommittee on foreign espionage was highly sceptical of Edmonds's allegations: one member remarked that they 'were regarded almost as the aberration of minds suffering under hallucinations', while another dismissed Edmonds as 'a silly witness from the [War Office]'.[7] Against this scepticism was concern that public worries had to be addressed. The subcommittee duly recommended that a secret service bureau be established with a domestic and an overseas department – this was the foundation of MI5 and MI6 – and that the Official Secrets Act of 1889 be overhauled to curtail the publication of sensitive information in the press.

Within the decade, the British intelligence community had grown from a handful of underfinanced spy catchers into 'a vast intelligence-gathering network, costing hundreds of thousands of pounds a year, and collecting information on virtually anyone opposed to government policy'.[8] From the basic provision of maps to naval commanders sailing to the Crimea to the surveillance of strategically located toilets (in 1884 the offices of the Special Irish Branch were destroyed when Fenians planted a bomb in the public urinal beneath it) the usefulness of security and intelligence activities soon became apparent.

Even so, a strong abhorrence of spying persisted, a distaste that had much to do with the secretive and unaccountable nature of intelligence activities. In 1908, Secretary of State for War, Viscount R.B. Haldane said that 'officers of all nations, when abroad, look about for useful information I have no doubt. But that ... is a different thing from coming as spies.'[9] Philip Knightley has shown that spying was (and still is) viewed officially as 'a dirty business more suited to foreigners than to Englishmen'.[10] But since the situation demanded that the British state stoop to similar methods, as far as was practicable it was desirable that such activities take place on an unofficial basis. Thus the state set up security and intelligence services that could be dissociated from government departments and shrouded its plans to register aliens in secrecy. The regime of the secret state was thus constructed in a way as to allow the government to deny its existence.

The populist fear of a German invasion provided the climate that the government needed to legislate tighter security measures and, in the wake of the Agadir Crisis, the government introduced new legislation. The summer of 1911 was a period of high tension between Britain and Germany. In June the Germans sent a gunboat to Morocco; a month later, Lloyd George publicly warned Germany of the risk of war. The new Official Secrets Bill had been introduced into the House in May, and on 25 July it was discussed in the House of Lords. It was presented by the War Minister, Haldane, who stressed the need to strengthen national security in the face of external threat. He claimed that the purpose of the bill was 'not to enact any large body of new restrictions, but to make more effective the law as it was intended to be made by the Official Secrets Act of 1889'.[11] To underscore the type of threat that Britain was encountering, he presented recent scenarios in which the existing act had failed: a man found in the fortifications at Dover claimed he was listening to birds; another man found looking at battery guns said he was calling on a friend nearby. The implication was clear: the enemy was about, gathering intelligence, and the present law was powerless to stop them. The press, which had objected so strongly in 1908, now offered little resistance.

Despite the assurances that the bill offered nothing new, there were significant changes. The leaks section was extended to include recipients as well as disclosers of information, a provision that would directly affect the press. In a wide departure from normal legal practice, the burden of proof was thrown upon the individual. The provisions concerning public access to proscribed areas was widened – a private dockyard where a government ship was being built was now out of bounds. Finally, the terms of arrest were loosened, bringing them into line with the procedures used in other felonies, and the power of search was introduced.[12]

A month later the bill returned to the House of Commons for its second reading. Again an effort was made to downplay the nature of the changes presented while the national security angle was stressed. The Attorney General added that there 'was nothing novel in the principle of the Bill'. Still, there was some hesitation. One MP was 'distressed' ... 'at the way that this Bill is going through – a Bill which would have been all the better for a detailed examination'. The government insisted that haste was necessary:

> It is undoubtedly in the public interest that this Bill should be passed, and passed at once ... I therefore make the appeal frankly to the House that they should on this occasion, without regarding it in any way as a precedent, except for matters of great urgency, give this Bill the Third Reading.[13]

Within the hour, the Official Secrets Bill had become law.

With these new policies in place, the transition from an economy of secrecy based upon shared culture and values to one of formal legal-rational control had begun. The British citizen now lived in a state where disclosure of *any* official information without express authorisation was an offence; where the accused was guilty until proven innocent; where the 'right to know' resided only at the centre of the state; and where decisions about loyalty and threat could be taken by the elites – this at a time when alternative political discourses were emerging that had as their objective the empowerment of the demos. These alternative values were, by definition, deviant ones that could not be accommodated within the dominant culture. Within the new boundaries of acceptable political behaviour, individuals who held alternative values found it prudent to repress or abandon them.

The contemporary justification for the new national security regime stressed the state's need for legislation to combat espionage, but the effect was to maintain strict control of official information, to prevent its falling into hostile hands – hands that could belong to its own electorate as easily as a foreign power. The linkage of the national security issue with the problem of bureaucratic control proved potent. No one wanted to test the bounds of political freedoms if it meant a German takeover of the United Kingdom. In moving from a *de facto* culture of secrecy within the state to formalised rules, policy-makers invented a legal-rational secrecy which injected the subjective problems of loyalty and patriotism into the equation. While spying for the Germans was clearly treacherous, it was the state's new legal power to rule on less obvious offences against national security that was dangerous. National security was to prove to be a very elastic concept indeed.

The new secrecy regime – the Official Secrets Act, the setting up of the security services, the new methods for controlling the press – fundamentally redefined the relationship between official information, the government and civil society, legally privileging excessive secrecy over open government. Traditional practices rooted in the elitist nature of the British state were placed onto a legal-rational footing. In this way, those within the state were able to perpetuate their own sociocultural biases, legitimating them through reference to the legal-rational state and to the need to safeguard national security. The accomplishment of this transformation from a state apparatus in which secrecy was a sociocultural value to a formalised bureaucratic regime was made possible by the linkage of the state's growing desire to control the dissemination of information to wider public demands for strong national security measures. The government, while less concerned about external threat, was anxious to reassert its failing ability to control its civil service and hence official information. In a state long used to the internal freedoms from accountability that secrecy made possible, the new winds of openness were chill indeed.

CHAPTER 3

INVENTING THE ENEMY 1919–1945

Threat assessment between the wars

In the early years of the twentieth century the verities of traditional realist diplomacy still obtained. Territorial borders demarcated the extent of national domains and foreign policy remained an elite sport; in terms of national security, the ultimate role of populations was to serve as cannon fodder in the war games of the rulers. The advent of ideologies and democratisation led to a reconfiguration of the role of the individual *vis-à-vis* the defence of the realm. In an era of total war and totalising beliefs, the individual no longer stood apart from the national security concerns of the elites, but became the focus of that concern: she or he was no longer a docile, submissive subject but a potentially powerful, potentially subversive force within the state, carrying the contaminants of socialism, nationalism, fascism, pacifism, or any other of the myriad dangerous ideas that were gaining currency.

To protect the status quo from these new political challenges, policy-makers at the centre sought to reassert their control over the political landscape by privileging those discourses that supported the existing distribution of power and marginalising and discrediting those that challenged it. This was accomplished by a mass mobilisation of the population in which national security became the private concern of each individual and each individual became the potential subject of the state's gaze. Through systems of surveillance, the classification and criminalisation of categories of political discourse and extensive control over the production and dissemination of information, the British state created a disciplinary regime in which the subject was culturally, morally and legally inducted into participating in the defence of a realm defined by and for the elites. A self-conscious leviathan within a monolithic British state did not *per se* exist; this new regime was the *effect* of numerous and disparate policies, not a specific objective.

Between the wars, state control over information began to operate at both overt and covert levels which fed into this changing national security regime. Overtly, through the policies that the centre chose to make visible to the demos, the population was intimidated by the spectacular and arbitrary application of the Official Secrets Act and other national security laws. After the war, the state's powers had been substantially strengthened by amendments to the OSA, its willingness to use the OSA increased and its definition of threat – that is, what discourses and activities the centre considered dangerous to the safety of the state – was extended. These changes were demonstrated regularly in the courts for the edification of a population that might be tempted to stray beyond acceptable political boundaries. At the covert level of state policy, the population became the subject of the activities of state apparatuses which scrutinised, recorded and classified individuals according to secret definitions of threat and loyalty. The security and intelligence services worked to shape these perceptions, using the information they assembled to create categories of acceptable political discourse which were then packaged as the national security demands of a legal-rational state. National security thus became the rationale for a totalising strategy of state control over information in which the ruling elites generated mechanisms by which to control and limit pluralistic political discourses. This strategy was two-pronged: on the one hand, information was gathered about the population; on the other, information was disseminated to engender certain attitudes and beliefs among that population.

As territorial boundaries ceased to serve as meaningful limits to the nation-state, governments faced new problems. National security issues increasingly bled into the issue of controlling populations. The power of state borders to serve as metaphors of citizenship was eroded by challenges posed by new doctrines. Ideologies by their very nature transcended state borders and undermined the simple us/them binary of citizenship that had served as a basis by which to identify the enemy. In Britain, the 'other' had spoken with a German accent, but doctrines like Irish republicanism and international socialism transcended state boundaries and undermined simplistic notions of loyalty based upon belonging to a particular state. The task of protecting the realm became twofold: first, policy-makers had to decide on the boundaries of acceptable political discourse in the absence of simple definitions based on citizenship; second, they had to develop mechanisms for policing those boundaries.

The growing awareness that democratic states had to appear to be protecting the rights of citizens in order to maintain political legitimacy conflicted with national security demands which could most effectively be met if such rights were curtailed. Britain was not alone in struggling to find a balance between individual freedom and national security. Canadian internment of the Japanese during the Second World War and American McCarthyism in the 1950s are examples of how democratic input can occur in the form of mass prejudice and is no more likely to protect individual rights. British policy-makers had their own experience of populist agitations: widespread fear of a German invasion had been a decisive influence on prewar policy.

In post-First World War Britain, literacy, democracy and education increasingly empowered the demos, its political consciousness tempered by the revolutionary experience of total war and accompanying dramatic social change. Books, newspapers and the airwaves, the rise of trade unionism and the women's movement and especially the relatively recent phenomenon of the ballot box gave the once puissant masses new voices. The elite sought to control this polyphony of discourses, rightfully fearful that its own preponderance over the governance of Britain might be under threat. The First World War had whetted the elite's appetite for power. It now found that by maintaining its preeminence over national security policy-making it could shore up its power over the stirring demos by inventing new concepts of citizenship.

Given the centralised and stratified nature of the British state, with political, economic and social power firmly concentrated at the centre, the elite's power to supervise political discourse was already advanced and its strategies of social control sophisticated. It became a relatively straightforward matter to transmogrify elite interests into the interests of the state writ large through the establishment of a new national security regime. Policies had to be convincingly justified to an electorate growing in size and sophistication. The legal-rational state provided a legitimating framework for the state's virtually total autonomy in national security policy-making. The need to protect the state from 'threats' was privileged over the emerging political freedoms of the individual.

Thus policy-makers engineered the carrying over of wartime practices directed against a German 'enemy' to a peacetime focus on the British population itself. National security was extended into everyday life with postwar amendments to the OSA and the increasing power of the security services being used to carry through and justify particular political agendas. The combination of excessive secrecy, spectacular punishments and wide-ranging surveillance contributed to elite preeminence in national security policy-making, with the demos cast in the role of an acquiescent and fearful audience upon which these new policies were enacted.

Before and during the First World War, OSA prosecutions were based on a still-recognisable concept of national security; one need only look at the names of the defendants in OSA cases – Heinrich Grosse, Max Schultz, Karl Graves, Karl Ernst – to have an accurate idea of who was being targeted under national security laws. By the 1920s, policy-makers themselves were no longer sure about what constituted threat. There was disagreement at the centre, for example, about the extent of the Soviet threat. In the cabinet, Conservative Party 'diehards' were inclined to feel the battle to save Britain was only beginning, a view they shared with powerful business interests and the security services. Other politicians were not so much soft on communism as sick of war, unenthusiastic about waging a battle against their own populace, however militant, and were concerned to get the British economy back on its feet – a project that trade with the Soviet Union could only help.[1]

Writing about the national security policies of China's Ming dynasty, the builders of the ultimate monument to national defence, the Great Wall, Arthur Waldron argued that 'if one wants to paint one's opponents as traitors, one's task is made easier if one can narrow the definition of patriotism'.[2] In essence, this is what the British security and intelligence services set out to do. In an era of unstable governance and uncertainty – the 1920s were characterised by shifting coalitions and floor-crossings in Westminster – the security and intelligence services' anti-Bolshevik ethos remained constant and eventually succeeded in filling the vacuum created by the absence of a clear peacetime agenda.

Following the end of the First World War, the security and intelligence services, which had grown rapidly during the war years, found themselves redundant, their budgets slashed. In need of a new *raison d'être*, they set about inventing a Bolshevik threat, glimpsing the hand of the Soviet terror behind the civil disturbances of the 1920s. The wartime director of Naval Intelligence, jobless in 1919, warned that 'Hard and bitter as the battle has been, we now have to face a far, far more ruthless foe, a foe that is hydra-headed and whose evil power will spread over the whole world, and that foe is Russia.'[3] Anti-Bolsheviks became increasingly concerned about residual state sympathy towards the left and worried that elected governments were not rising to meet the challenge of the communist enemy within. Lloyd George was bombarded with reports from the intelligence community that prophesied nothing less than 'revolution in this country and that before 12 months are past'.[4]

While Lloyd George and others remained sceptical, the security and intelligence services were already taking the initiative in drawing up new categories of threat. Soon, merely being tolerant of the left was transmuted into evidence of incipient disloyalty. Lloyd George was branded a traitor by no less than the chief of the Imperial General Staff; when Ramsay MacDonald came to power, he asked to see his security file and was refused; and Stanley Baldwin was regarded by Special Branch as soft on communism because he would not ban the Communist Party.

For the rightwing in general and the security and intelligence services in particular, those who were not part of the solution were part of the problem. With national security being thus constructed – leftwing activities attributed to Soviet incitement and tolerance of such activities portrayed as support for the enemy – the rightwing succeeded in coopting the security agenda. Soon this influence would made itself felt in specific policy decisions.

A spectacular security culture

If the enemy was really 'within', then the subject's role in national security was no longer one of simply presenting arms when arms were called for. Citizens were now required to participate permanently in the protection of the Britain state by circumscribing their own behaviour and being suspicious of the behaviour of others. The state used the OSA and other laws to create an overt, visible security culture designed to demonstrate to the population the political boundaries it must keep itself within. The policy-making centre disseminated its new definitions of loyalty through the state's ideology-dispensing apparatus and policed this definition through the legal system. The OSA became the central legitimising plank in the creation of this 'spectacular' security culture, spectacular in the sense that the state produced and stage-managed spectacles or events in order to demonstrate its power and its will. The population was reminded of its obligations towards the security of the state through regular public displays of the legal-rational power invested in the OSA.

Although reluctant to crack down on the left *per se*, postwar governments were willing to augment the state's security powers by carrying over the lessons of the war into peacetime, starting with the amendment of the OSA and the introduction of an Emergency Powers Act in 1920. These new security laws were joined in the coming decades by the Trades Dispute Act (1927); an Incitement to Disaffection law (1934); a new Public Order Act (1936) and numerous measures to curb rising violence in Northern Ireland.

Under the terms of the 1911 OSA, all official information was defined as being subject to the control of the state. To divulge, seek or acquire official information, to be alien, to fraternise with 'potential' or actual enemies of the realm, even to be careless or indiscrete, had been categorised as suspect and in some cases criminalised before the First World War. Nevertheless, the OSA had mainly been used in cases where a particular action could be clearly seen to jeopardise national security. After the First World War the ambit of the OSA was extended and categories of acceptable behaviour narrowed to a point where it was virtually impossible to guess what sort of action might be considered threatening – a reflection of elite uncertainty about the future nature of threat. An influential rightwing condominium of interests emerged between the security and intelligence services and sectors of an elite that was beginning to regard certain kinds of legitimate participation in the political life of the state as animated by the Soviet menace. Thus whole categories of behaviour and discourse, mainly on the left, were classified as threatening to the state.

The 1920 amendments brought deep changes to the OSA. The most significant change concerned the rules governing evidence: from 1920 it was possible to bring a case under a lesser section 2 (unauthorised disclosure) charge if there was insufficient evidence for an espionage prosecution. Unlike section 1 (espionage) charges, there was no legal test in section 2 to determine whether the disclosure of official information was prejudicial to the interests of the state, although, initially at least, the judiciary attempted to throw out cases which did not directly concern national security. The judiciary was nominally independent of political influence (although its overwhelmingly upper-class bias located it firmly within the establishment), but it proved to be in thrall to elite guidance on national security issues. Judges found that they could not convincingly challenge the centre's agenda even if they wanted to because the centre alone was permitted to rule on national security issues. If the government claimed that a given action was threatening, the judiciary was not in a position to cavil. Cases that judges threw out were on occasion resubmitted by Attorneys General, who frequently undertook prosecutions personally to underscore the importance the state attached to these seemingly trivial matters.

To extend the power of the OSA into non-national-security cases it was necessary to establish a legal-rational context in which such applications would be tolerated by the judiciary, the press and the general public. There were a number of tactics that prosecutors used to deflect attention away from the fact that 'espionage' laws were being turned against those who should have been considered 'loyal' citizens. One method was to double up charges: defendants were frequently charged under both the OSA and laws concerning corruption or confidence, or, if they were in the military, under both military and civilian law. A raft of charges intimated the general baseness of the defendant – it was easier to paint someone as disloyal if they were also portrayed as corrupt. A typical example involved the conviction of an Air Ministry clerk who in 1928 offered to sell details of rival firms' bids and contracts to a competitor. He was found guilty on both section 2 and corruption charges and sentenced to two months concurrent on each charge.[5]

Doubling up of charges also made a kind of 'plea bargaining' possible: defendants were threatened with felony and espionage charges and encouraged to plead guilty to lesser counts. In 1934 a section 2 charge was brought against a civil servant at Woolwich Arsenal who offered to sell Imperial Chemical technical information concerning an explosives contract the company had applied for and lost.[6] The defendant claimed he would rather cut off his right hand than do anything to harm the security of the state; he simply needed some money. A witness from the Arsenal said the documents contained test results that could have been arrived at by anyone conducting the tests; the judge and the prosecution agreed that the offence was not serious. However, the judge ruled that, because the disclosure could save a theoretical enemy time and effort, it was prejudicial to the state. The civil servant received a twelve-month sentence, a ruling indicative of how elastic the idea of national security had already become.

Another tactic was the regular use of *in camera* trials, another new power introduced by the 1920 amendments. The public naturally assumed that the matters being tried *in camera* must involve state secrets – for why else would public justice be waived? – while the state was saved having to attempt to justify its use of the OSA to a potentially sceptical public. *In camera* trials enabled the state to display to the public a relationship between national security and official information which it did not have to justify or explain; it was thus able to retain its preeminent position over national security matters. For example, in 1927 a retired naval officer was convicted in a secret trial when, two months after his retirement, some plans were found missing.[7] The proceedings of this case, which falls under the 75-year rule regarding disclosure on national security matters, will remain secret until 2002.

To help buttress its attempts to widen the power of the OSA, the government frequently sent its Attorneys General into court to argue cases. The authoritative arguments of a bewigged minister, representing as he did the monopoly on national security information held by the government, helped persuade judges and juries, the media and the public of the seriousness with which the state regarded transgressions. Seemingly trivial disclosures could be implied to be threatening to the state. In 1926 the governor of Pentonville Prison found himself facing the Attorney General in the courtroom, his crime having been to write up the lurid deathbed confession of a murderer on the eve of his execution and sell it to a newspaper.[8] The case was a watershed: Major Blake's defence argued unsuccessfully that section 2 should only apply to disclosures that were prejudicial to the interests of the state. The court found that all official information was covered, regardless of its classification or confidentiality, and the Attorney General took the opportunity to remind publishers that newspapers could be prosecuted for handling illicit information.

In 1932 that threat was acted upon. A temporary clerk gave the details of three celebrity wills to a journalist just a few hours before they were due to be officially released; for this unauthorised disclosure, the journalist was sentenced to two months in prison, the terminally ill clerk six weeks. A former Attorney General argued an appeal on the basis that the leak could not possibly be considered inimical to the interests of the state, but the appeal failed. He was countered by serving Attorney General Thomas Inskip, who said it was a matter of principle: 'the defendant has carried on this tampering with the official sources of information to the prejudice of trade competition and the corruption of the civil service'.[9] National security had now been stretched to include protection of the state from corruption and trade competition – an astonishing extension of its meaning.

The demos lacked alternative information about national security; it was forced to rely upon the state's own presentation of how matters stood and had no reference points external to the centre's own views of loyalty and threat. To legitimate and publicise the new security culture, the state began to mount show trials. OSA offenses became excuses to mount sensational trials designed to remind the public that the enemy was everywhere but the state was vigilant.

The 1933 trial of Seaforth Highlander officer, Lieutenant N. Baillie-Stewart, combined the elements of public spectacle and utter secrecy that characterised the overt/covert national security regime.[10] Amidst highly publicised accusations of espionage committed during a sexual liaison with a woman from Berlin, Baillie-Stewart was held in the Tower of London, a move designed to cast him as a very public enemy. The bulk of the trial, however, took place *in camera.*

Baillie-Stewart was charged under both the OSA and parallel court martial regulations, a seamless legal net in which he had little hope of escape, despite the shakiness of the prosecution's case. Baillie-Stewart was accused of selling to German agents, among other things, a picture of a supposedly secret tank which had in fact been paraded publicly. The defence insisted that Baillie-Stewart's only 'crime' was to have had sex with a German woman. Four generals, nine colonels and 61 officers testified to his reliability. During a closed session, the prosecution produced its *coup de grâce,* Baillie-Stewart's confession to Major 'A', a confession given in return for a promise that he would not be convicted. Instead Major A became a key prosecution witness and Baillie-Stewart received a five-year sentence.

Similar cloak-and-dagger trappings surrounded the 1938 trial of the Woolwich spy ring. MI5 agent Olga Grey began her penetration of the Communist Party of Great Britain (CPGB) in 1931 and discovered that a former Woolwich Arsenal employee had convinced three fellow employees to supply information which he then passed on to the Soviet Union. When Grey unmasked the ring in 1937, the four members of the ring were charged under section 1. The case took place in the utmost secrecy. The hearing did not appear on the list of cases being heard, the press was not allowed to see the charge sheet, and, on the opening day of the trial, the police waited for the court to be cleared before it led the four accused into the dock. Grey, appearing under the pseudonym 'Miss X', initially gave her evidence *in camera,* although it was subsequently revealed in open hearings. The defence attacked the trial procedures as unduly sensationalist but the Attorney General, appearing for the prosecution, argued that tight security arrangements were necessary to safeguard the nation's security.[11] He was not required to offer any further justification for the secretive tactics employed.

A show trial of a different sort involved the celebrated author Compton Mackenzie, who was convicted of making unauthorised disclosures in his war memoirs in 1933. The state had begun to take a hard legal line against authors in 1921, when it took issue with a former civil servant's book about the Supreme War Council. The book utilised a number of official documents. The Prime Minister noted that, while no 'dangerous treachery' was involved, the practice was unacceptable and all civil servants were required to seek explicit permission from the government for publishing works related to their service to the Crown.[12] This policy was applied haphazardly. In 1923 a small parliamentary storm blew up after Winston Churchill was not charged for writing a newspaper article that clearly utilised official information.

Mackenzie's *Greek Memories* concerned his experience in intelligence work in Athens in 1914. Although Mackenzie's book utilised secret documents, the prosecution did not emphasise the national security aspects of the case; instead, the Attorney General stressed that the case was to serve as a warning to those 'whose urge to write is greater than their discretion'.[13] The son of former Labour leader George Lansbury was convicted of a similar offence in 1934 when he published a biography of his father based partly on official documents. Attorney General Inskip made the state's position crystal clear: 'the Official Secrets Act must either be, as far as possible, enforced or it must be treated as a dead letter'.[14] Enforcement, however, stopped short of the source of the documents, George Lansbury, who happened to have served as leader of the opposition.

Official secrets trials were at the forefront of the state's strategies to legitimate its use of political power. Through moral persuasion and backed by legal coercion, the public's role in national security was to obey and to participate in, but not to question, elite dictates. The state enshrined in law the moral responsibilities of loyalty and patriotism; established its monopoly over official information, thereby asserting its omnipotence in national security matters; inculcated a chilling effect on the general population and the press through arbitrary usage of powers of arrest and prosecution which blurred the lines between legitimate, criminal and traitorous actions; and orchestrated spectacular displays of its power which exhibited to the demos its overt national security regime.

During the interwar years the state increasingly employed the tactics of the spectacle to suggest to the population how the interests of the centre and the margins coincided in struggling to defeat external foes. This overt attempt at legitimation masked a growing divergence between the security policy that the government was willing to present to the demos and the policies it was actually pursuing. Through spectacle, the state tried to engender a fear of an 'other' who was increasingly hard to recognise.

The covert national security regime

Policy-makers, while endeavouring to protect the British population from this 'other', underwent a perversion of their own view of this objective: from the centre, it increasingly seemed that it was the general population that was threatening and that it was the centre that needed to be protected – a logical enough extension of the traditional elite fears of the masses. The grafting of a Bolshevik menace onto traditional fears was combined with the cooption of the security agenda by the rightwing; together these drove forward the centre's ability to use legal-rational means to limit political discourses in new ways.

The political executive was already losing its power to control the national security agenda to the security and intelligence services. Within the policy-making milieu it was the secret services who wielded the practical powers of surveillance and classification of the population, and armed with such information they were able to claim authority in the policy-making discourse of threat assessment. Just as the population at large suffered from having no external references for comparison, policy-makers were to a substantial extent beholden to the information and perceptions supplied by MI5 and MI6.

The security and intelligence services' war against subversion quickly outpaced the broadening of the legislated security agenda. Their operations were driven underground as their actions became increasingly dubious in terms of both legality and the targets against which they were directed. Persuaded by the security and intelligence services, the centre seemed content to acquiesce in the subversion of legal process given the exigencies of a national security situation they did not entirely understand.

As a result, the battle with Bolshevism increasingly encompassed the British left, with intelligence-targeting skating ever closer to recognisably legitimate political groups. Disinformation, dirty tricks, smears, harassment, raids and surveillance became the stock-in-trade of the security services, which by the 1920s had crossed into the nether world of illegality and unaccountability. Its political masters, depending on its individual fears of Bolshevism, either found that extraordinary threats justified extraordinary actions or, with the distaste of the Victorian gentleman and/or acute political instinct, preferred not to know. Elected policy-makers abnegated responsibility for civil liberties, aware that, in protecting individual rights in an era of uncertain danger, one could easily find oneself accused of protecting the enemy.

By the 1920s, the espionage section of the OSA was seldom used and then mainly against amateur spies and corrupt civil servants. German state-organised espionage in Britain scarcely existed, and as late as 1939 the sorts of espionage cases being tried suggested only an opportunistic German effort. In November 1938 a Vickers-Armstrong engineer was imprisoned for three years for obtaining a plan of a fuse-setting machine, but he had not been in contact with any enemy agents; a year later a Lancashire man received ten years on five section 1 charges for selling RAF plans to the Germans.[15] British counter-espionage was no better at catching spies than the Germans were in providing them. Most information came from alert citizens who tipped off MI5 about possible spies. A former German army intelligence officer was caught in 1935 when his landlady complained to the police that he had not paid his rent.[16]

Threat within the British state between the wars emanated from the left, from the right and from the Irish cause rather than from Germany. The Irish threat posed a particular set of problems which characterised the dilemmas posed by policing internal subversion. The identification of potential subversives involved the security and intelligence services in designating certain groups and organisations as 'suspect' and placing them under surveillance. By birth alone the Irish became potential threats to the state, the more dangerous because distinguishing between the violent nationalist enemy and everyone else was impossible without making assumptions that would infringe on civil liberties.

The Irish were ubiquitous in the mainland labour force and as such had access to all sorts of nooks and crannies of the British state. A wave of violence erupted in the turmoil surrounding the 1916 Easter Rising and republicans had little problem infiltrating and subverting British intelligence-gathering and counterespionage efforts. Several months after a 1920 operation in which the IRA moved against twenty leading British secret agents, killing thirteen and injuring six, two IRA moles were recruited instantly when they presented themselves to a British official claiming to hate Sinn Fein and need money.

The espionage provisions of the OSA did not apply to Irish subversives because the Irish were not considered 'the enemy' under the terms of the Act. The problems this caused first surfaced in the 1920 trial of IRA sympathiser Michael Simington, an employee at the Office of Works, who was charged with a section 2 offence for unlawfully retaining plans of the Irish Office in Westminster and of buildings used by the Ministry of Munitions' explosives departments. Although he was committing an espionage offence, section 1 required that information be useful to an enemy and the British state was reluctant to classify the Irish legally as such. Section 2 allowed for a lesser charge to be brought against Simington and he received a 15-month sentence. A similar case occurred in 1925 when a civil servant and a shipwright were charged under sections 1 and 2 following the arrest of five IRA members for spying around the Portsmouth Dockyards. The leader was an IRA intelligence officer who was supplying information on a top secret naval experimental tank, and it was rumoured in Dublin that the IRA was planning to blow up the HMS *Monarch*. He pleaded guilty to a section 2 charge and received a comparatively light sentence of 18 months.

But it was the Bolsheviks, not the Germans or the Irish, that the security and intelligence services were most worried about. Concrete examples of Soviet spying remained rare as the game of espionage and counterespionage was still comparatively undeveloped. Britain was a target for Comintern aid and support and Cheka intelligence operations, but the extent of their influence was already limited by the numerous laws concerning subversion, sedition, trade disputes, fraternising with foreign agents and so on. Furthermore, it was virtually impossible for a Russian to impersonate a Briton and thus penetrate British intelligence. A secret Comintern international liaison department began recruiting party members and fellow travellers into secret service work in 1921, but Soviet espionage did not really get off the ground until the early 1930s, when Soviet recruiters began to connect with political sympathisers on the university campuses, a policy that would pay dividends as the Cambridge Apostles moved into positions of influence. Bolshevik support in the 1920s was largely confined to providing political and material support.

Nevertheless, the threat of communist subversion was built up to further the interests of hardliners within the British policy-making elite. The covert side of national security operations was occasionally fed into the public arena in order to legitimate policies that were highly controversial. The first attempt to use the Soviet threat to create public support for a contentious policy occurred in 1928 in a case involving an English underwriter, Wilfred McCartney, and his Soviet controller, a German student named Georg Hansen. This was the first case of Soviet espionage brought to court in Britain, and is an early example of an intersection of the public face of espionage – a public criminal trial – and the ultrasecret machinations of the security and intelligence services. The whole point of the case was to engineer a crisis that would allow Britain to sever diplomatic ties with the Soviet Union.

In 1927 McCartney, a former army intelligence officer, was working as a rather incompetent spy for the Soviet Union, admitting himself that his espionage operations exhibited 'cretin-like stupidity'.[17] Seeking information about an arms shipment to the Soviet border states, McCartney attempted to bribe Lloyds insurance broker George Monkland. Monkland immediately contacted the authorities and became a double agent for MI5, providing false information to McCartney, who was placed under MI5 surveillance.

This occurred at a time when, in the cabinet, rightwing diehards were trying to engineer an opportunity to sever relations with the Soviet Union. To justify a break publicly they were looking for a scandal on the scale of the 1924 Zinoviev letter, a document supposedly written by the president of the Comintern. The Zinoviev letter – a forgery – had urged British communists to prepare for the revolution through their work with the armed forces and their sympathisers in the Labour Party. Published four days before the General Election, the letter was generally held to have caused the Labour Party's defeat at the polls.

In their search for a similar scandal, the diehards were assisted by the security and intelligence services, which offered up proof of Soviet treachery as it became available. The diehards were gradually gaining the upper hand in a cabinet stalemated on the Soviet problem. The cabinet had already sent a protest note over the Soviet promulgation of anti-British propaganda, warning that relations were under threat. The Russians counterattacked, accusing the British government of mounting an anti-Soviet campaign, and demanding evidence in place of smears and insinuations. Monkland, the diehards hoped, might supply such evidence.

Through Monkland, MI5 planted an RAF manual on

McCartney, who passed it on to a member of the Soviet trade delegation, which was housed at Soviet House with Arcos, the joint-stock trading company and the suspected nerve centre of Soviet espionage activities. Then MI5 presented its dossier on McCartney to cabinet as concrete evidence of Soviet spying. On 11 May the Home Office authorised a raid on Arcos, intending to recover the 'secret' manual they had planted on McCartney and thus furnish proof of espionage. The police carried off hundreds of thousands of documents which, The Times reported, showed that 'behind a large and no doubt legitimate trade organization, the Soviet Government were conducting in London an international campaign for the overthrow of institutions'.[18]

However, the irrefutable evidence did not emerge (the manual was not recovered), leaving the government in the position of lacking any real evidence to justify the raid. Panicking, the cabinet resorted to admitting publicly that the state had been intercepting Soviet telegrams. Prime Minister Stanley Baldwin read out some of the telegrams to the House, providing 'proof' of Soviet treachery, and relations were broken off. But as far as British counterintelligence was concerned, the political triumph of the hardliners had exacted a terrible price. Following the exposure of the security service's telegram-interception operation, the Soviets immediately changed their communications codes and cyphers. These proved to be unbreakable, depriving the security services of their major source of high-grade intelligence. Furthermore, even the intercepts contained little convincing evidence of espionage, allowing the Soviets to score a propaganda victory over the underhand methods of 'the gentlemen burglars in London'.[19]

McCartney was finally arrested in November and tried the following January. McCartney's evidence suggested that Soviet espionage in Britain was more developed than was previously thought and the detailed knowledge he possessed pointed to a civil service leak somewhere. Already it was obvious that the state's efforts to safeguard national security were failing to staunch the flow of information leaking out to 'the enemy', despite the introduction of sweeping powers. It was also obvious that the era of the Victorian gentleman spy was truly over: covert operations would be used to legitimate political agendas and civil rights were irrelevant to the battle against the Bolshevik menace.

The fight against the left and the state's growing disregard for legal process continued apace. A disturbing case arose in 1937 when the state launched a prosecution against Wilfred Vernon, a long-serving technical officer at RAF Farnborough, whose legitimate political activism led to persecution, smears and finally trumped-up criminal charges.[20] Vernon was a committed socialist and a member of the Labour Party. He had been involved in a study group at Farnborough and had formed a self-help group for the unemployed which was officially disapproved of and finally disbanded.

Vernon's bungalow was burgled, and a number of classified documents and books were stolen. Four men associated with British fascists were charged, but the burglary was almost certainly instigated by the security services. At their trial, the burglars successfully presented themselves as patriots. The chief defendant, an army deserter and ex-IRA member, argued that Vernon was a Communist Party member who had incited him to desert and admitted to the court his purpose in committing the burglary was to acquire evidence for the security service. Although convicted, the four were given very lenient sentences, being simply bound over for twelve months. Vernon was then charged under the OSA for unlawfully retaining official documents. The prosecution alleged that Vernon had neither the right to retain or even look at some of the secret documents in his possession. The defence pointed out that out of 100,000 words of official material taken, only about 200 words could be considered classified. Vernon received a £50 fine plus costs but, more usefully from the security services' point of view, was dismissed from the civil service for his offence.

The most compelling demonstration of the state's willingness to manipulate evidence and engage in covert operations in pursuit of political objectives came about in 1940 when Tyler Kent, a code and cypher clerk at the American embassy, and his contact Anna Wolkoff, a rightwing activist, were charged with espionage.[21] Gillman and Gillman have argued that Kent and Wolkoff were pawns in the effort within hardline sectors of the British government to introduce mass internment, a move being resisted by Home Secretary Sir John Anderson. The timely arrests of Kent and Wolkoff provided the trigger for the round-up of British fascists desired by the cabinet hardliners fighting Anderson's position.

Tyler Kent served in the American embassy in Moscow from 1933, where he lived extravagantly, giving rise to subsequent speculations that he augmented his income through cooperation with Soviet intelligence. In 1939 Kent was transferred to London where he made copies of secret correspondence between Roosevelt and Churchill, intending to use it to undermine Roosevelt's upcoming bid for re-election. Soon after his arrival in Britain, MI5 placed him under surveillance because of his contacts with a Gestapo operative and his association with the Right Club, an anti-Jewish society headed by Conservative MP and former Director of Naval Intelligence Captain Maule Ramsey. Ramsey believed there was a conspiracy of Jews, Bolsheviks and Freemasons trying to take over the world.

Anna Wolkoff, whose parents owned the Russian Tea Rooms where the Right Club met, introduced Tyler Kent to Ramsey. Kent showed Ramsey some of his illicit documents and Ramsey considered tabling a parliamentary question concerning the extra-official embassy traffic. MI5 agent Joan Miller had penetrated the Right Club and knew Anna Wolkoff was in contact with the Italian military attaché, fifth columnists and Kent. However, as Andrew Lownie notes, MI5

> continued to monitor Kent and say nothing. There is no indication that the American authorities were informed of the code clerk's activities, which is surprising given that MI5 quickly discovered that Kent was copying highly secret cables. It may have been that the British needed to collect evidence against Kent, or that MI5 did not feel they could pass on their 'intelligence' without the risk of it being compromised.[22]

In cabinet, Anderson continued to argue that the Right Club and similar associations, including Oswald Moseley's British Union of Fascists, did not pose a threat sufficient to justify the internment of their leaders: 'Although the policy of the British Union of Fascists is to oppose the war and to condemn the Government, there is no evidence that they would assist the enemy', he wrote. 'Their public propaganda strikes a patriotic note.'[23]

But within cabinet, hardliners were once again hunting for enough evidence to justify a change in Anderson's 'soft' policy and it was thought that an OSA case might provide the vehicle. Hoping to achieve an espionage conviction, Wolkoff was set up by MI5. An MI5 operative asked Wolkoff to use her connections with the Italian military attaché to send a letter to Lord Haw-Haw. She passed the letter on to another member of the Right Club who claimed to have access to the Romanian diplomatic bag, but who was another MI5 agent. The agent suggested Wolkoff add her own note to Lord Haw-Haw and even provided the typewriter. Wolkoff wrote the letter and gave it to the MI5 agent, thereby handing over 'proof' that she was a foreign agent.

From mid-April there was enough manufactured evidence to charge Kent and Wolkoff with treason but no move was made to arrest the pair. Instead they were kept under close surveillance, but neither seemed to be behaving in a threatening or dangerous manner. Gillman and Gillman argue that the timing of the arrests belies the political intriguing in the cabinet that led to Churchill taking over from Chamberlain in early May. Emergency legislation had been drawn up by 1937, which included a detention clause so harsh that its architects in the Home Office decided to wait for hostilities before making the provision public. When Germany invaded Poland, the Defence Regulations were issued by an Order-inCouncil, including a regulation allowing the detention of people who posed a potential threat to public safety as well as those who were actively engaged in prejudicial activity.

After parliamentary protests, the regulation was watered down, but cabinet hardliners continued to push for stronger measures. Such measures were still being opposed by Anderson at the Home Office and also, interestingly, by MI5 head General Vernon Kell, who maintained that the most serious threats to British security had been rounded up in the September 1939 sweep. At a cabinet discussion on 18 May, Anderson still balked at initiating a round-up of fascists, but, even as he did so, the security services were calling on the American Ambassador to request that Kent's diplomatic immunity be waived. On 20 May Kent and Wolkoff were arrested, and by 22 May the new mass detention regulation was issued. Within two days, 59 people were rounded up and imprisoned, including Oswald Moseley, Captain Ramsey and other prominent fascists.

Still fighting mass internment, Anderson tried to have Kent deported rather than tried, but he was once again thwarted by the hardliners who wanted an impressive conviction in order to justify their round-up of British subjects. Much of the committal proceedings and virtually the entire trial of Kent and Wolkoff were held in such secretive circumstances that even Kent's mother had difficulty in finding out what had happened to him.[24] This secrecy suited powerful American interests in Britain who, like the British, were supporting the re-election of Roosevelt.

The Kent-Wolkoff affair was made to look like a straightforward case of German espionage. Kent was charged with offences relating to four documents. He insisted he had only committed a misdemeanour and protested that the selectivity of the documents on which he was prosecuted distorted his real agenda, which was not German espionage, but isolationism:

I have been tried on the basis of documents selected for the purposes of the Prosecution, taken from a group of over 500 other documents which were in my possession ... The jury has been asked to determine so subjective a thing as my intent with regard to those four documents, and they have had no opportunity of seeing the four documents in their proper light, namely against the background of the total sum of documents which are in my possession.[25]

Kent was given seven years hard labour and Wolkoff received ten years hard labour. Later evidence concerning Tyler Kent suggests that he might have been a Soviet mole; he was patently not the German spy he was portrayed as at his trial.

The Kent–Wolkoff arrests marked the turning point in the careers of Anderson and Kell, who rapidly lost ground to the hardliners. By 27 May, Kell had been replaced by his second-in-command, Allen Harker – a close friend of Joseph Ball, who acted as liaison between MI5 and Neville Chamberlain. (Gillman and Gillman speculate that it was Ball who alerted Chamberlain to Kent and Wolkoff in the first place and that it might have been Harker who ordered their arrests even as Anderson stone-walled.)[26] Anderson managed to survive in the War Cabinet until October.

For a society to consider itself politically 'free', the espousal of alternative versions of governance is a fundamental right, a right that is frequently problematic as it requires the balancing of the good of society as a whole against the freedom of the individual. In the British case, throughout the interwar period, a covert and totalising paralegal web of surveillance, espionage and threat perception animated a security policy that increasingly circumscribed political freedoms, limiting and essentially criminalising subjects for falling – deliberately or inadvertently – into categories deemed threatening.

Assisted by the new security and intelligence services, right-wing policy-makers acquired the processes of information production, organisation and distribution which allowed them to defeat their liberal opponents based on their 'superior' information, creating a climate in which smears, innuendo and paranoia posed as genuine evidence of threat. The elites inevitably became victims of their own closed policy-making process. By placing the surveillance and classification functions into unaccountable hands of the security and intelligence services, policy-makers lost their control of their own monopoly on national security information.

Intelligence in the new era of totalising ideologies had its own internal dynamic which mitigated against debate: feeding on uncertainty and paranoia, the covert power of British security services grew stronger. Where their mechanisms of surveillance and classification dovetailed with elite prejudices, the power of the state was tipped towards protecting that state *from* its citizens rather than towards protecting its citizens.

Parameters of political discourse were built up through accretion rather than by design, the product of myriad policy decisions and prejudices over decades. It could not have been the intention of policy-makers to create a national security leviathan that would ultimately consume its own elected representatives, but this was the consequence of the interwar reconfiguration of national security, which tilted the balance heavily against open government and accountability. Legislation purporting to protect official information was increasingly used to cloak establishment and particularly security and intelligence service prejudices against the left. With the reorientation towards an internal enemy and the lack of accountability for actions carried out 'in defence of the realm', the policy-making centre allowed political freedoms to be sacrificed on the altar of national security.

CHAPTER 4

THE FAILURE OF COLD WAR SECURITY

There is a terrible truth about the security services; I mean, we believed for twenty-five years that if you were an old Etonian, you could not be a traitor.

Roy Hattersley[1]

In a world riven by opposing ideologies, national security ceased to be a case of protecting the nation state; the possibility of a genuinely democratic 'national' security that took into consideration the needs and desires of the entire population rather than those of a select few policy-makers disappeared with the onset of the Cold War. National requirements were subsumed by the defence needs of two superpower blocs locked in global competition and British policy-making was increasingly driven by the American view of the world. There were tensions and differences about how best to meet the Soviet threat, but policy debates generally involved means, not ends. The strategic objective – Soviet defeat – was not in question.

This new objective was grafted onto the existing assumptions about British security which posited unimpeachable loyalty at the centre of the state and potential treachery within the demos. The declaration of war on communism, its source now clearly identified as the Soviet Union, gave British policy-makers the tangible and unambiguous external threat they had long sought. There was no longer any need to appear apologetic about targeting the left since such policies now took place within the context of a Western effort to defeat Stalin's expansionist totalitarian regime.

Populations were increasingly regarded as a resource, much like geostrategic advantage and nuclear prowess, things that could hamper or assist the eventual defeat of the communist menace depending on how they were deployed. The watershed example of this is perhaps the American defeat in Vietnam, where 'errors' in the handling of the population at home convinced many policy-makers that they were defeated not by the military prowess of the enemy but by American public opinion. This lesson was successfully applied later during Britain's Falklands adventure and again during the 1990–91 war against Iraq, where the Western media was strictly controlled. It has taken democracies like the US and the UK several decades to refine their methods of population 'control' via manipulation of national security information. Significantly, it was the Americans who learned much from the British example of the advantages that secrecy bestows upon governments in national security matters.

The development of postwar policy

The centralisation of the British state, the concentration of power in elite hands, long-entrenched secrecy and the habit of shutting out democratic participation in national security meant that mass campaigns similar to American McCarthyism did not occur in Britain. To mobilise the population into witch-hunts would mean delegating power to the demos and this was not the British style. The centre instead continued to follow its old custom of viewing its subjects with suspicion and setting its policies accordingly. Just as the elites were home to all that was loyal, the masses were the putative home of subversion, and the British elites had lengthy experience in dealing with subversives.

The wartime practice of rendering individual rights secondary to security exigencies was now extended into the uncharted terrains of fighting a Cold War. Where suspicions existed about an individual's 'loyalty', democratic states hit upon the formula that doubt should be resolved in favour of the state. When used in precisely defined circumstances and with a careful view to the protection of individual freedoms, such a formula was perhaps the best compromise that could be found, but in the UK it was too easily abused. The safety of the state quickly became an unassailable justification for the erosion of democratic rights. As the British internal security regime tightened in the immediate postwar period, the definition of threat became broader and civil liberties correspondingly imperilled. Draconian security laws were drafted and vetting, censorship, surveillance and the curtailment of political freedoms became common practice.

The practice of privileging state needs over individual rights in security matters was undermined by elite exceptionalism. Ultimately, the Old Boys network carried more weight than bureaucratic security arrangements. As the uncertainty and deepening paranoia of the 1950s progressed into the scandal-ridden 1960s, it became increasingly clear that the Soviet Union had penetrated to the very core of the British security state. British policy-makers, in positing their own loyalty as beyond question, had made a fatal miscalculation.

Even if alternative political discourses had remained fairly muted, under the widening security net more groups would have been stigmatised as threatening. However, the postwar era saw an escalation in the exercise of political rights. Ideologies were infecting everyone as decolonisation, socialism, opposition to nuclear weapons and the increasing polarisation between left and right raised rather than lowered consciousness. Resistance and agitation for change became both more common and more strident, and from the centre's point of view, examples of popular resistance began to look more and more like extremism. Positing that much of this activity was directed from Moscow, policy-makers felt justified in further tightening the security regime.

As a result, it was leftist, not rightist, activities that caused the most concern. As far as rightwing extremism was concerned, the 1945 Labour Government was content to continue wartime Coalition practices in its treatment of fascists and nazis. The Home Secretary's position was that fascism should not be outlawed: 'freedom of speech' was more important, he felt, especially since there was little evidence of public support for fascism and such a movement was unlikely to flourish. While rudimentary surveillance was placed on British fascist networks, it was not considered sufficiently threatening to require any specific curbs. Instead, British intelligence found convenient allies among the anticommunist nazi collaborator networks in Europe which were quickly recruited to assist in the defeat of the Soviet empire.

The left, however, came under attack, even though the internal communist threat was perhaps equally insignificant. The likelihood of an indigenous socialist overthrow of the British state was remote and even Bolshevism's electoral prospects were dim. The U-turns and hypocrisies of Stalinist communism had alienated the majority of British adherents from the cause. In the 1945 general election the Communist Party won only two seats; in 1947 it was deemed too feeble to be allowed to join the Cominform, the postwar successor to the Comintern; and by 1950, 97 of the 100 Communist Party election candidates lost their deposits.[2]

Despite communism's lack of appeal in postwar Britain, this did not prevent the centre from eliding the indigenous leftist 'threat' into the external threat posed by the Soviet Union. Longstanding elite prejudices against the British left were now seemingly vindicated by the spectre of a Soviet hand behind them. The line between external threat and internal subversion became blurred as the state enacted measures against its own population under the guise of national security. The Labour Party expelled 'extremists' from its ranks and the Labour government introduced purge procedures into the civil service, enabling the state to remove civil servants suspected of having fascist or communist associations from sensitive posts. 'Suspicion' was sufficient grounds for gaining a transfer or dismissal; proof of disloyalty was unnecessary. While the definition included fascist organisations, in practice it was the suspected communists who were purged; Hennessey and Brownfeld note that 'The security authorities were overjoyed when they eventually found a fascist in one of the service departments. It made the whole operation look even-handed.'[3]

The threat posed by the Soviet Union was another matter, and was genuine. In September 1945 Soviet cypher clerk Igor Gouzenko defected in Ottawa, taking with him documentary evidence of Soviet penetration of the transnational atomic weapons research programme. With Gouzenko's evidence MI5 was able to identify British physicist Alan Nunn May, who passed atomic secrets, including samples of uranium-235. Convicted under the OSA, Nunn May received a ten-year sentence. A second atomic spy, Klaus Fuchs, also came to light, and received a 14-year sentence.

This opening salvo in the spy wars planted seeds of distrust among the Western allies. Suspicious of British security practices, the US severed connections between British and American atomic research after August 1946. British security had been a relaxed affair: membership in the Old Boys network usually provided the open sesame into top secret work, and good 'chaps' were not seriously suspected of being capable of treason. Both Nunn May and Fuchs were known to harbour communist sympathies but had been cleared by MI5 to work on top secret projects associated with the Manhattan Project.

The extent of the failure of British security policy would become more evident as the Cold War deepened. Policy-makers were unwilling to undertake the kinds of uncomfortable security measures that would have placed the loyalty of the establishment under scrutiny; indeed, they were apparently unable to accept that individuals within elite ranks were capable of disloyalty. Disloyalty was invested in the population, not within the establishment; it always involved 'them', never 'us', and it proved

easier to define oneself as 'in' by defining everyone else as 'out'.
With an eye to convincing the Americans – and themselves – of
their trustworthiness, British policy-makers found the best way
to remain above suspicion was to sport anti-Soviet credentials.
Thus while British fascists were left largely unmolested, vetting
and purges were directed against leftists.

British policy-makers are frequently applauded for their
avoidance of American-style witch-hunts, but entrenched elitism
in recruitment practices at the centre of the state ensured its
continuing homogeneity, making large-scale civil service purges
unnecessary. That only 25 British civil servants were dismissed
from their posts, compared to 9,500 in the US, is frequently
misleadingly cited as evidence of the liberal nature of the British
response. However, in a secretive state, it was easy for policy-
makers to hide the extent to which civil liberties were being
betrayed. In the US, 'traitors' were publicly exposed; in Britain,
those who fell under suspicion remained anonymous. Quiet and
informal action was preferred to officially orchestrated and public
campaigns, resignations and blocked promotions preferable to
noisy purges.

The great irony of course was that security was compromised
less by offenders at the margins than by the secretive and insular
nature of the British establishment itself. So predictable was the
path to political power that the KGB used Oxbridge as a recruiting ground for future spies. A combination of class, school and
social loyalties and an unnerving complacence in its own ability
to judge the reliability of its members led the ruling establishment to overlook security risks in its own ranks. It continued to
represent itself as the repository of all that was good and loyal in
the British state, even as it harboured the most nefarious and
successful Soviet agents – Donald Maclean, Guy Burgess, Kim
Philby and Anthony Blunt. When the first two went missing,
there were no attempts to propagandise the fact that sons of
Cabinet Ministers, bright Cambridge graduates, and/or ranking
Foreign Office officials could be spies. Instead, the media questioned how violent drunkards with psychiatric problems and
communist pasts had survived so long in the Foreign Office, but
the government remained outwardly sanguine.

Genuine efforts to uncover what was wrong at the centre of
the British state would open a Pandora's box of sticky questions
about the elite's method of rule, where recruitment, advancement
and protection still relied more upon family ties than rational
governance. And so, as Lord Annan writes,

> The Establishment closed its ranks. The security services had to be cleared of the charge of incompetence and Foreign Office of negligence. The Establishment was determined not to allow [media baron] Beaverbrook to play the role of Senator McCarthy and cause droves of innocent men and women to lose their jobs through guilt by association.[4]

The British horror of unleashing a witch-hunt was used to justify the centre's do-nothing policy. What the establishment feared, however, was not witch-hunts, but exposures that might challenge its primacy in the British political order. The only real subject of a witch-hunt was Burgess's close friend Goronwy Rees, principal of University College of Wales, Aberystwyth. His sin was not that he was procommunist, but that he wrote articles suggesting that maybe it was the centre, not the margins, that needed to be purged of traitors. Annan writes: 'the explosion detonated by these articles was atomic. But the blast walls of the Establishment are so cunningly constructed that the person most hideously wounded was Goronwy Rees himself.'[5] A purge was indeed initiated, not against suspect elites, but against Rees, whose suitability as Principal was questioned in a formal enquiry. Although no evidence emerged that this 'consort of Burgess' was unreliable, Rees was thoroughly discredited and resigned. Not only this, but Annan notes that Rees was excluded from fashionable dinner parties henceforth.

The expansion of security and intelligence service activity is well documented; the effects of security policy on the general population is less well understood. The official secrecy record reveals some of the effects that the legal manifestations of the new security agenda had upon the body politic. Elite attitudes to security veered from the draconian to the lenient without any apparent reference to the potential or actual consequences of security violations. The real victims of British security policy were those without powerful protectors in the establishment and unable to arouse the sympathy of the press. While those who were excluded (as opposed to actively and systematically purged) through elite prejudices cannot be traced, the OSA provides some empirical evidence as to how the security agenda worked against the margins and was used to ensure the centre's primacy.

During the war years there were numerous security-related prosecutions under the OSA, the Defence of the Realm Act and other defence regulations. Such prosecutions dropped off immediately after the war: aside from the two atomic spies, only a Polish national was charged (and convicted) of espionage, though of a minor sort. There were two non-espionage cases between 1946 and 1950, involving four defendants who committed minor indiscretions and received small fines. In one case a military intelligence officer and a reporter were convicted in a magistrates' court for collaborating on a story, and in the other a reporter and a telephone operator were fined following a story about a police identity parade.[6] The prosecutions were petty, the punishments insignificant.

While there were moves within the Labour Party, the government, the civil service and the security and intelligence services to attack the Soviet Union through the British left, this shift was not immediately evident through the public medium of the courts. In 1949 China was 'lost' to communism; a year later, the war in Korea broke out and doubts and fears about the Soviet menace intensified, yet the OSA was still seldom used against leftists, although it was used to attack those who sought to question official policies. In 1951 three men were each fined £50 for exchanging secret information about military aircraft, information they intended to use 'to applaud or criticize the government'.[7] The prosecution claimed that the case was not subversive and the trio's fines were reduced to £10 on appeal. As late as 1956, a former civil servant who tried to incite a junior in the Department of the Director of Ordnance to sell him 'secrets' – he wanted to write an article exposing wastefulness in government – received a small fine.[8]

Espionage was regarded seriously, but in the early 1950s paranoia had not yet bitten deeply and the relative forbearance accorded the atomic spies continued into the 1950s. In 1952, William Marshall, a radio operator at the Foreign Office, was jailed for five years on espionage offences. Serving in the diplomatic wireless service in Moscow, Marshall was an ideological spy but not an important source of information, and the jury specifically asked for leniency.[9]

A hardening regime

Within a few years such leniency was disappearing. By the end of the 1950s, the courtroom was increasingly the forum where the state established the notion that all information was of potential value to an enemy and, more importantly, that individuals lacked the ability to make judgements about their actions. Unauthorised disclosure was an absolute offence. It was not information per se that mattered to the state, but the mere fact that an individual had disclosed it. This constituted a monumental shift of democratic power from the citizenry to the state as the individual was essentially categorised as disloyal if he or she divulged any information.

While this was the natural continuance of pre-Second World War attitudes to security, it was strengthened by the presence of the communist threat and the bureaucratic apparatus set up to deal with it. The OSA had bestowed upon the state the twin mechanisms of surveillance and spectacle and now the Soviet threat was used to justify increasing surveillance of leftwing British groups and a more generalised intrusion of state surveillance into the lives of individual Britons, especially those with access to official information. All individuals were vulnerable to persuasion and corruption, but, under the guise of establishing a secure civil service, the state bureaucratised its prejudices against the demos. Sexual orientation and behaviour, religious and moral beliefs, family and acquaintances, all became matters of national security which were recorded in the vetting files of the security and intelligence services, thus enmeshing the citizenry in the state's national security regime.

Spectacular and arbitrary punishments for leaks coexisted uneasily with the state's efforts to appear competent in matters of national security. Infractions that should have been punished were covered up, while others that were relatively minor were dealt with harshly. In 1956 security officers approached Anthony Wraight, a flying officer with the RAF, about his contacts with the Soviet embassy. Within the week Wraight had defected to the USSR, slipping out of the hands of the security services. In 1959 he returned to England, where he was interrogated for three weeks by civil authorities and released. He then audaciously published his memoirs in a Sunday paper and it was only in the wake of this public admission of his spying that the state finally acted. Wraight was eventually convicted of both section 1 and section 2 offences for which he received a 'salutatory' sentence of three years, with the judge admitting that the offences were not serious.[10]

Such arbitrariness made it more difficult for individuals to make judgements about their actions vis-à-vis the national security regime, but it was not until the late 1950s that the depth of the sea change taking place became apparent. A number of 'deterrent' cases were prosecuted where harsh punishments were handed out for violations that did not jeopardise national security, but that signalled to those with access to official information that breaches would not be tolerated. The number of cases and the length of sentences skyrocketed. A two-year sentence was the maximum penalty for a section 2 (unauthorised disclosure) violation. In 1958 a 20-year-old assistant test manager at a defence establishment, suffering from psychological problems, received the maximum sentence when he tried to sell details of munitions tests and contracts to a man he met at a labour exchange.[11] The same year, another two-year sentence was handed down to an RAF clerk who was found with documents concerning surface-to-air missiles. There had been no evidence of an attempt to divulge the documents and furthermore the officer in charge attested that they were of no importance.

Technically, this sentence reflected the defendant's attempt to escape arrest, but much was made of the fact that the clerk had 'signed the Act'. People in contact with official information were routinely required to sign a standardised undertaking indicating that they were aware of the provisions of the OSA. 'Signing the Act' was of great rhetorical but little legal value, since one did not have to be aware of the OSA in order to be bound by it. Yet those who had signed the Act earned the maximum opprobrium for they were painted as being guilty of moral as well as legal indiscretions. Not only had they misused official information, but they had *promised* they would not.

When building prosecution cases against those suspected of section 1 (espionage) offences, there was little effort made to distinguish between 'legitimate' leftwing politics that might challenge the status quo and genuine Soviet subversion. Nor was the extent of the damage caused to British security necessarily seen as a mitigating factor when it came to sentencing. The *maximum* sentence for an espionage offence was 14 years; the *average* sentence passed between 1946 and 1988 was 14 years.

Professional Soviet spies tended to draw significantly longer sentences: for example, the Portland spy ringleader Gordon Lonsdale, a Soviet deep-cover agent, got 25 years while the agents he recruited drew 15 years apiece. Such harsh penalties were ameliorated by the genteel practices of spy swapping, immunity deals and so on, with Eastern Bloc agents held in the West exchanged for Britons held in the East. Anthony Blunt was offered not only immunity but also a knighthood. Burgess, Maclean and Philby made good their defections, and, with a kind of divine justice, Soviet mole George Blake was sprung from prison by two antinuclear campaigners who were also serving sentences for espionage.

The first major public controversy over where the line between legitimate dissent and treachery should be drawn occurred in 1958. The notoriety of the *Isis* case possibly derived from the fact it involved two Oxford students – Britain's future elites – who published an article based on their experiences during National Service. The students had served in the Royal Navy Special Reserve where they had been taught Russian and then sent to Germany to eavesdrop on Soviet signals communications. Their article, which appeared in an issue of *Isis*, the Oxford student paper, and which was then picked up by the national press, discussed the ostensibly secret General Communications Headquarters (GCHQ) listening post at Cheltenham. The students described Anglo–American efforts to gather information on Soviet military manoeuvres by penetrating Eastern Bloc airspace and waters and then recording the Soviet response. They wrote:

> this flagrant breach of the Geneva Convention can provide accurate estimates of the size and type of Russian armaments and troops, and the nature of their tactical methods ... After the war a fleet of half-a-dozen exceedingly fast Mercedes-Benz torpedo-type boats were built and, manned by sailors from Hitler's navy, were sent out under English Captains to provoke and listen to the Russians.[12]

The *Isis* case underscored the vulnerability of the state's ability to control information. Individuals, particularly in the military, were the Achilles' heel of British security and were targeted by Soviet intelligence who used blackmail and money in order to seduce would-be agents. While concerns about Soviet entrapment were legitimate, the state's greater concerns lay in the fact that civil servants and military personnel could reveal information in order to advance political objectives such as nuclear disarmament. One of the *Isis* students remarked to the police that the publicity stirred up by a prosecution would only help their cause.

The case became a spectacular prosecution designed to remind those with access to official information of their duty to be silent. The prosecution did not base its case on a national security breach; it did not need to. There was ample evidence that the students had committed a technical breach of section 2, and, furthermore, they had 'signed the Act'. Nevertheless, the case provoked a controversy because the article had not undermined security. The defence proved that the information the students had divulged was well known and much of it had been published previously in the United States.

The court, however, upheld the state's monopoly over control of information. Although it was objectively true that information was already in the public domain, this was incidental, for the implication was that it might just as easily not have been; loyal subjects were silent and discreet, accepting that, as they did not know Soviet or British intentions and plans, they could not reasonably judge what it was safe to divulge. The trial judge, Lord Goddard, made this point crystal clear: 'It is not for young men employed in these matters ... to decide for themselves what is vital to the security of this country, and what secrets must be maintained.' The pair were convicted and sentenced to three months. However, an elitist double standard saved the Oxbridge students from the worst of their punishment: Goddard backdated the sentences to the start of the trial – during which they were bailed – and recommended it be served 'in the most favourable circumstances', in an open prison, which he hoped would 'keep them away from criminals'.[13]

The OSA was fast becoming an extremely reliable method of enforcing the sanctity of government control of information; once charged, it was very difficult to escape conviction given the technical interpretation of the Act. There were occasional remarkable exceptions, but acquittals were regarded as anomalies. One such case involved Dr Giuseppe Martelli, an Italian physicist working at the Atomic Energy Authority, arrested on a tip-off in 1963 from a KGB defector. An amateur spy with no access to classified documents, Martelli was arrested with all sorts of espionage paraphernalia, including shoes and cigarette packs with concealment cavities in them, cipher pads and records of meetings with KGB officers. The jury acquitted him on the basis of such compelling defence arguments as that the abundance of circumstantial evidence could be explained by the fact that Martelli liked to play spy games with his son. Although Martelli's contract with Euratom was suspended, he was given a clean bill of health and not deported.[14]

Acquittals under the OSA were so rare that they led to internal security crises whenever juries returned them, as in the Martelli case. Even with the state's monopoly over national security issues and the stringency of the OSA, occasionally juries or judges would buck the trend and find a defendant not guilty. From the centre's point of view, such verdicts did not suggest that defendants were innocent or the security services slipshod in their cases. Acquittals only emphasised that juries – and by extension, the general population – could not be trusted in national security matters. The acquittal of Martelli was not a vindication of a justice system that threw out cases where the evidence was not compelling, but a confirmation of elite fears that the demos was soft on communism. This drove the centre to further extremes of secrecy involving security and intelligence service operations where evidence was shaky. When convincing cases could be built, these were turned into public spectaculars, while more serious potential cases were swept under the carpet.

The double standard tended to favour the more powerful elites who were near the centre of the state, while those who committed offences but lacked powerful protectors paid the price of the harsh security regime. A number of allegations emerged about Soviet spies in the House of Commons, but no MPs were ever convicted. In 1970 William Owen MP was acquitted for lack of evidence.[15] Owen had been recruited by Czechoslovakian intelligence and was discovered when two defectors revealed his treachery. For a retainer of £500 a month, he fed information to the Czechs for fifteen years and was well placed to provide valuable information, having been at one point a member of the Commons Defence Estimates Committee. The prosecution failed to prove that he had passed any information and the defectors' evidence was inadmissible. Owen resigned his parliamentary seat and confessed to MI5 on the promise of immunity.

The defectors' information alleged the existence of other spies in the Commons but cases against three other Labour MPs were not proceeded with because of the difficulties demonstrated by the Owen case. John Stonehouse, formerly Minister for Aviation, Postmaster General and Minister of Posts and Telecommunications, denied MI5's allegations and the matter was dropped. Tom Driberg also passed on secrets to the KGB, and was turned into a double – or even triple – agent. At least one other MP-turned-agent was never identified.

But in the majority of cases a charge almost always meant a conviction and the state's stepped-up pursuit of deterrent cases continually sent the message that individual conscience or judgement in security matters was intolerable. In 1962 Barbara Fell OBE, a 23-year veteran of the civil service working at the Central Office of Information, received the maximum two-year sentence for unauthorised disclosure. Fell had supplied the press councillor at the Yugoslav embassy, with whom she was having an affair, with confidential information. The information included reports from the British Ambassador in Belgrade to the Foreign Secretary. The documents were of no security value and only one was classified. Fell argued that her lover was politically reliable and that she only showed him the documents to guide him. She had the interests of the state in mind when she did so: 'I care deeply for my country and believe in its democratic institutions and way of life and government. I would do nothing to harm its interests or endanger its security.'[16]

A leave to appeal was denied and the procedural irregularities of the case ignored. Fell had been interrogated daily by intelligence officers and was not allowed to see a solicitor; she had cooperated fully and the only evidence presented against her was her own confession. Fell's lawyers argued that the judge had not paid enough attention to the fact that security had not been jeopardised, but the appeal court stressed that a section 2 offence was 'absolute and is committed whatever the document contains, whatever the motive for disclosure is and whether or not the disclosure is prejudicial to the State. The essence of the offence is the disclosure of confidential information.'[17]

An all-party committee moved that the Royal Prerogative of Mercy be recommended and there were calls to cut the sentence to three months. These attempts to get Fell off the hook are suggestive of how those near the centre of the state were more likely to be protected by the establishment. As a long-serving senior civil servant, Fell was deemed to merit the benefit of the doubt, unlike more marginalised disclosers. But the decision to prosecute indicated that even senior mandarins with impeccable characters were not fit to make individual judgements about the use of official information. Appeal judge Lord Parker summed up this position when he said 'The higher one's position, the greater one's responsibility.'[18]

In 1961, in a new manifestation of the Cold War climate of harshness, the state charged six peace activists with espionage. Six antinuclear campaigners belonging to the Committee of 100 were charged under section 1 when they peacefully occupied a military airfield. The accused used the 'interests of the State' clause of the OSA to challenge the state's own nuclear policy, arguing that it was the presence of nuclear weapons on British soil that represented the greatest threat to Britain's security. The court quickly disallowed this line of argument and the defendants were sentenced to between 12 and 18 months in prison.

The sentences were upheld on appeal, but the appeal court did ask the House of Lords to clarify the meaning of the phrase 'purpose prejudicial to the safety or interests of the State'. The subsequent rulings underscored the slipperiness of the wording. The Law Lords decided that 'State' could mean 'the realm' or 'the organised community' – that is, the state writ large – or the term could more narrowly refer specifically to 'the organs of government of a national community'. Given the OSA specifically concerned national security, it was the latter definition that obtained, as only the Crown had the prerogative to make national security policy. Therefore, Lord Devlin explained that the statute was not concerned with 'what the interests of the State might be or ought to be but with what they actually are at the time of the alleged offence'. While the 'interests of the State' might sometimes diverge from the 'interests of the community', the OSA was not the law under which to challenge such anomalies. 'This statute is concerned with the safety and interests of the State and therefore with the objects of State policy, even though judged *sub specie aeternatis*, that policy may be wrong.'[19]

As the security scandals of the 1960s began to emerge, the state's treatment of offenders grew more draconian. Until 1961, the atomic spy Klaus Fuchs was the only person to receive the 14-year maximum sentence for espionage. But in 1961 MI6 double agent George Blake was unmasked. Blake's greatest espionage coup was his compromise of the CIA's Operation Gold, a 1950s attempt to dig a tunnel from West to East Berlin, allowing the Americans to intercept KGB and military signals traffic. Thanks to Blake, the KGB knew the Americans were listening in and provided eleven months' worth of disinformation before the operation was blown.

When confronted, Blake confessed almost immediately to being a Soviet agent and pleaded guilty in a trial that lasted less than a day. The revelation was in the sentencing. The judge condemned Blake to three consecutive and two concurrent 14-year sentences, adding up to an unprecedented 42 years in prison. Its harshness actually created a degree of public sympathy for Blake; in an appeal it was argued that in practice Blake's sentence exceeded a life sentence because he would not be eligible for Home Office review. The sentence was upheld.

With Blake's appeal dismissed, the 14-year ceiling on espionage sentences was smashed and long sentences were routinely passed. This new harshness may have been a result of the numerous security scandals of the 1960s: the credibility of British security and intelligence was eroded by the defections of the Cambridge Apostles, the exposure of Blake, the Profumo affair and a constant stream of espionage prosecutions. The state hit back with a series of spectacular punishments designed to cow the population into silence, even as members of the elite who caused the major damage managed to elude British justice. Amateur spies on the margins of the state suffered disproportionately. Many received long sentences for inept and thoughtless crimes that did not jeopardise security.

The Blake saga was quickly followed by the trial of the Portland spy ring. Accounts published before the 1980s suggested that a sharp-eyed naval security officer uncovered the ring when he made enquiries about why Harry Houghton, a clerk at the Admiralty Underwater Weapons Establishment, could live so well on his meagre salary.[20] In theory, this is how the new security regime should have worked; the intrusiveness of surveillance might have been justified if it indeed netted spies. In practice, however, the tip-off had come from Polish defector Michal Goleniewski, who had also blown the whistle on Blake. It was only on Goleniewski's information that MI5 placed Houghton and his girlfriend, a fellow employee, under surveillance and found the pair consorting with Gordon Lonsdale, a Canadian playboy-businessman who was a deep-cover Soviet spy. The police pounced on the pair as they handed over a shopping basket full of secret documents to Lonsdale. The police also moved in on other Lonsdale associates, the Krogers, a couple who had fled the US when the Rosenberg spy ring was discovered. The Krogers provided technical support and communications facilities for an unknown number of Soviet agents in the UK.

Lonsdale, as the head of the spy ring, received a 25-year sentence, while the Krogers, as professional spies but not instigators, received 20 years apiece. However, being members of the spy world's elite, these professional Soviet agents benefited. In 1963 Lonsdale was swapped for British businessman Greville Wynne, who was serving an espionage sentence in the USSR, and the Krogers were exchanged in 1969 for a British lecturer. Houghton and his girlfriend received shorter sentences, but spent more time in British prisons, not being released until 1970.

The discovery of a spy ring at Portland created a panic which led to official investigations into security lapses. Houghton had been a Writer to the Naval Attaché in Warsaw and had been transferred back to the UK in 1952 because of his dissolute behaviour, which included heavy drinking and carousing, carrying on black market trade in coffee, and having an affair with a Polish woman. It was during this period he was recruited by Eastern intelligence. The eventual report on the matter was strongly critical of naval security and it led to the setting up of a new Security Department in the Admiralty.

The creation of a spy-proof military, civil service and research and development environment was proving impossible, though civil liberties and principles of justice continued to be trampled on in the wake of such scandals. Vetting, surveillance and dubious security service operations were permitted even when these were failing to protect the state from enemy penetration. With secret cameras, a spy did not need to remove sensitive documentation, and, even if under constant surveillance, an employee could not be prevented from using his or her own eyes, ears and memory to retain information that could later be leaked, sold or publicised. Some offenders signed out files and documents to which they had legitimate access; others simply removed documents improperly.

Vetting also failed to detect potential offenders. Many crimes were committed impulsively, sometimes after years of loyal service. In 1965 Sergeant Peter Allen, attached to the War Office, received ten years for a section 1 offence. His wife was tested for cancer, and although the tests proved negative, Allen became obsessed with the idea that she was dying. With four children and heavy debts, he was scarcely behaving rationally when he stole secret documents and sold them to the Iraqis for the princely sum of £75. Ironically, Allen was reputed to be particularly strict on security matters and he had been inspired to commit his offence by a War Office lecture on security. The Security Commission concluded that

> Allen's essay in espionage was impulsive and amateur. He was not attracted to it by ideological sympathy, nor forced into it by fear or compelling financial need; still less was he lured by mere cupidity. The margin by which he became a spy must have been small.[21]

Nevertheless, vetting continued to be used and abused by the state. While it could not prevent Soviet penetration, it did enable the state to deny entry into the ranks of the civil service to those it did not think fitted the image of the loyal Briton. Large-scale vetting programmes were used to screen out potential risks, with little defence available to those denied jobs or promotions for reasons that they never knew. At the same time, the official regime was eroded from within the armed forces and the civil service by the Old Boys networks, which continued to protect insiders. Successive scandals followed by security commission investigations showed again and again that colleagues who were obvious security risks were often shielded. It is difficult to draw a line between what was protection through old ties and what was simply incompetence. At any rate, the scandals of the 1960s belied a complaisance about security within the state which was publicly obscured by spectacular examples such as Allen's ten-year sentence for a minor offence.

The security service intrusions into the interstices of Britons' lives also yielded little in the way of detecting Soviet moles. Spies were almost always discovered through contact with defectors and double agents rather than through surveillance. The legal system could not be always be worked to the state's advantage because of the illegality and inadmissibility of evidence about many Soviet spies. The case of William Vassall was an example of the gap between theory and practice in security procedures. An 'obvious' homosexual, Vassall was nevertheless recruited to the Admiralty after the war and in 1953 was sent to the Naval Attaché's office in Moscow. Moscow quickly entrapped him in the Soviet espionage net through money and incriminating photographs. By 1955 Vassall was supplying minor documents from his office to the Soviets, who photographed and returned them. In 1956 Vassall was returned to London where he assisted in the office of the Civil Lord of the Admiralty – again, not a very useful position, but Moscow continued to pay him. Their patience paid off, for in 1959 Vassall was posted to the Secretariat of the Naval Staff and was given access to valuable military information. He was exposed by the defection of Anatoliy Golitsyn to the US in December 1961 and in 1962 was sentenced to 18 years for his offences.

The official line was that Vassall had been caught following increased security in the Admiralty after the Portland and Blake cases, a cover story that not only protected secret service operations but also conveniently hid the failure of existing security practices. Vassall had been positively vetted according to the prescribed procedures, but either his homosexuality was not discovered or not deemed important. The Tribunal of Inquiry convened to examine security breaches following the Vassall case found this 'disquieting' and decided that errors of judgement had been made.[22] The press was scathing. A *Times* editorial criticised a security regime that apparently allowed homosexual bachelors living beyond their salaries to serve in sensitive posts. While the balance between civil liberties and security was difficult to strike, *The Times* suggested that 'those who engage in secret work must resign themselves to a degree of encroachment upon their private life; or it must be accepted that the safety of the country is constantly at risk'.[23]

The media eventually succeeded in forcing Vassall's former employer, Undersecretary of the Admiralty Thomas Galbraith, to resign over accusations that Galbraith knew Vassall was a spy and/or was involved in a homosexual relationship with him. The government, characteristically less concerned with slipshod security arrangements than its reputation, counterattacked. The Radcliffe Committee was set up to review the role of the press in the affair, diverting attention away from the security failure and towards the issue of press–state relations. After twelve days of taking *in camera* evidence, the Radcliffe Committee concluded that the press stories were not justified, thus absolving the government of blame.[24]

Vetting failed again in 1965, when an engineer in the Ministry of Civil Aviation was convicted of espionage.[25] Heavily in debt and with a criminal past, Frank Bossard was recruited by the Soviets in 1961. Bossard worked in guided missiles research and development, costing and programming weapons, but did no technical work, nor did he have access to top secret materials. He did not even require security clearance for this post, although he had been positively vetted for his earlier signals intelligence (sigint) work. It is not clear what he had passed to the Soviet Union; even Lord Parker seemed vague, telling Bossard 'What damage you have done ... no one can tell', before handing down a 21-year sentence.[26]

The review of the case again revealed glaring errors of judgement. Bossard had been positively vetted even though officials knew he had lied about his criminal record when he applied to join the Ministry. The vettors argued that Bossard had been imprisoned for six months some 18 years previously and, as his service record caused no complaint, they considered him rehabilitated. However, since he had lied about his past, the Security Commission found that Bossard was unreliable by definition and should not have received a security clearance.[27]

In 1968 Douglas Britten was found guilty and sentenced to 21 years. He was an RAF chief technician with a history of financial problems. Again, he had been security vetted twice and was not considered a risk. He was recruited by the Soviets in 1962 and supplied them with classified sigint for the next six years. The Security Commission investigated the case to see if vetting should have identified Britten as a risk and decided that vetting was developed as a screening process, not a way of catching spies: '[Britten] was evidently a good actor and an accomplished liar', it concluded. 'When such a man decides to betray his country, he indeed presents the security authorities with a formidable problem of detection.'[28]

In 1972 the Security Commission was convened to investigate vetting procedures following the conviction of Sub-Lieutenant David Bingham, who received a 21-year sentence for his essay into naval espionage. Chronically in debt, it was Bingham's wife Maureen who approached Soviet intelligence and arranged for her husband to sell information. Bingham spied for 18 months before finally confessing to his commanding officer. Bingham's financial troubles had come to the attention of his superiors on two previous occasions. Both times, the matter was not felt serious enough to report to the Directorate of Naval Security. The Security Commission concluded that there had been no particular security lapse in not reporting Bingham, but found that the case:

> points to the need for a wider recognition of the fact that an individual's financial difficulties ... may indicate a vulnerability such as Bingham's. In case of doubt the superior officer should not hesitate to report them promptly to the security authorities.[29]

Maureen Bingham, who asked the Soviets for legal aid to save her husband and spent some time in a mental hospital, was charged under the OSA for incitement after she admitted publicly that she had been the instigator of the espionage. She was sentenced to two-and-a-half years.[30]

Unmasking KGB spies legitimised the activities of MI5 and MI6 and the trampling of civil liberties was justified by the exposure of Soviet treachery. But such exposures pointed more to the limitations of the measures being taken to protect the state. Vetting of civil servants failed to identify potential or actual spies, and intelligence operations were seldom successful in uncovering offenders. Most spies were discovered through their own errors or confessions, or through information from defectors whose evidence was virtually useless in a British court of law. Nevertheless, the practices of vetting and surveillance, the illegal activities of the security and intelligence services, the duplicity and double-dealings at the centre in protecting establishment figures and its own reputation, continued to characterise the security regime of the British state. Such measures undermined rather than supported British security; however, they did allow the centre to maintain its control over the definition of treachery. Even faced by the Soviet threat, British policy-makers chose to follow a self-serving and deeply flawed agenda that protected their own interests while it diminished the rights and freedoms of the general population.

CHAPTER 5

OFFICIAL SECRECY AND THE PRESS

> You'll never find in a British newspaper who meets whom. Not like in America – their papers are big-mouthed; we used to find out a lot from their Press. In England, no information could be found from the papers. I always taught my people: 'Do everything like the British.'
>
> former KGB chairman Vladimir Semichastny [1]

The British media context

Despite its notoriety, the Official Secrets Act has contributed surprisingly little to media constraint. In popular mythology the OSA represents the apex of the British state's practices of secrecy and censorship, but in fact it is far less important as a mechanism of information control than as a rhetorical device. The early twentieth-century move to legally control official information was accompanied by the formalisation of outlets so that information could still flow, albeit now through the channels inscribed by a legal-rational state. Lacking alternative sources of official information and increasingly hemmed in theoretically by the widening judicial interpretation of the OSA, the media had little alternative but to comply with state arrangements. By doing so, they legitimated the system of information control that was being erected.

Journalists, critics and scholars have focused on the legal-rational processes mandated by the OSA and by doing so have amplified a liberal model of adversarial state–media relations. However, an examination of the record of official secrecy cases involving the press suggests that this focus obscures the extent to which the media have actually supported and colluded with the centre's 'secret state'. The media have been more likely to contribute to, rather than mitigate, secrecy in Britain.

Western states accord the media a privileged place in the state–society relationship. In liberal political theory the role of the media is to act as the main channel of communication between government and civil society. It is a 'system which generates the information necessary for effective citizen control of politicians', and serves as 'a powerful extension of the accountability of governments'.[2] An independent press ensures that non-state agents – journalists, and, by extension, the citizens they represent – have power within the state. By providing a platform where alternative discourses can be engaged in and serving as a conduit between citizen and government, the media widen citizens' sense of participation in the life of the state and their sense of political efficacy. Liberty of the press is therefore considered sacrosanct, an essential element of liberal democracy.

It is generally accepted that this liberal model holds true for British politics. Media and government exist in a state of tension, with the media standing outside the state to interrogate and challenge the state's use of political power on behalf of the demos. On the one hand, this positing of a media/state binary gives credence to claims of an independent press acting as the peoples' watchdog; even the names of the various 'quality' papers underscore this role (the *Independent*, the *Guardian*, the *Observer*) or suggest an objective, non-partisan 'reporting' of what is going on within the state, enabling the citizen to be reasonably informed (*The Times*, the *Telegraph*). On the other hand, a state's claims to legitimacy in liberal democratic terms rests upon its respect for the fourth estate, a claim that can be undermined if the state curtails press freedoms. Media power flows from the media's role in legitimating the democratic state; this power sustains the tension between government and press.

The liberal binary is transmuted for the public's consumption into the structuring of a highly adversarial media–state relationship; the media, we are constantly reminded, 'act as the guardians of our unwritten constitution, continually invading and inspecting those spaces of society which by inertia and laziness we have allowed to go rotten, fighting government censorship all the way'.[3] During the storm over reporting restrictions during the *Spycatcher* affair a *Guardian* editorial argued:

> The idea that newspapers should be prevented from reporting facts ... could only be contemplated in a country where free speech is a legal 'left-over' – left over after the laws of confidentiality, contempt and secrecy have had their say. There is a serious hole in our domestic law which a genuine democracy would be eager to close: the absence of any legal provision guaranteeing free speech.[4]

Such quotations etch the liberal model more deeply into the national consciousness: newspapers are concerned with 'facts' and with the project of telling the truth, forcing governments to be accountable. The darker side of this implication is that governments are willing to attempt lies and cover-ups – in this example, the Thatcher government's legal battles to silence an exposé of MI5 dirty tricks – while journalists wear the proverbial white hats. Consumers of media messages are encouraged to believe that, in spite of official constraints, British democracy is healthy because the press is battling to push back the parameters of state secrecy.

In positing an adversarial model of media–state relations, this liberal binary is deeply misleading. Its widespread acceptance serves the needs of both media and government: the media assert their independence from the government by stressing their role as critics, while the state tolerates the 'independent' media, accepting them as the watchdogs deemed so necessary to accepted democratic principles. The structuring of media–state relations in this way diverts attention from the complex networks connecting the media and the state which jeopardise journalistic independence and thus the very underpinnings of British democracy.

The Official Secrets Act has played a subtle but vital role in the legitimation of this adversarial model. It symbolises the lengths that governments will go to in order to gag their journalistic foes and therefore obscures the extent of media–state collusion. That measures like the OSA are necessary implies that the media are a powerful check on state power, further enhancing the media's claims of independence and importance to British politics.

A key measure of the quality of democracy is how effectively the media represent the interests of the demos. As Marxists point out, the media as a capitalist enterprise have long been more concerned about making money than about protecting democratic rights. Their contribution to democracy has always been fatally compromised by their engagement in the cash nexus. In addition to the undergirding capitalist concerns of newspaper proprietors, however, the way in which access to official information has been structured in the British state has led the media to identify with policy-makers rather than citizens.

Media independence is compromised more deeply in Britain because of the state's success in controlling official information. Compared to other liberal democracies, the UK ranks low in terms of political transparency, access to information and protection of free speech. Excessive official secrecy has forced the media to work under constraints not found in other countries. To ensure access to sources, the media have reached an accommodation with the state, forging relationships with political and bureaucratic actors inside the policy-making apparatus. While the system is superficially adversarial, at a deeper level the mainstream media have been effectively coopted.

The representation of citizens' interests is compromised by the extent to which the media identify their interests not with the masses but with maintaining access to information controlled from within the state. While the media reflect a diversity of opinion, this apparent 'diversity' should not mask the actual narrowness of the debate. If media interests were aligned with citizens rather than customers, or with democracy rather than capitalism, the diversity of discourses of the demos might be represented more fully. Politicians and journalists regularly claim to desire freedom of information, but few actually wish to upset a system that both accords the media a politically and economically powerful position and suits the needs of the government. Within the elitist and exclusive policy-making milieu of the British state, media interests are invested in maintaining the status quo.

Journalists are more likely to share the views obtaining at the centre of the state than those at the margins, a shared elite vision engendered by general class, cultural, social and financial alliances. Editors and major journalists in the national press are as likely to be white male Oxbridge graduates as their governmental counterparts; they even join the same clubs (women journalists complain that their job is made difficult because they are denied access to the all-important sources of information only available through the Old Boys network). Incipient elitism at the top is refracted through the journalistic corps, where reporters regularly shape their stories to please their editors in order to get them into print, or to please their sources in order to ensure a continued flow of information. Policy-makers, naturally enough, are more likely to throw morsels of information to journalists they think will represent them most favourably, ensuring a narrowing of the coterie of successful journalists. And because they have been accorded the privilege of glimpsing the 'facts', journalists immediately vault over the demos in terms of the authority of their discourses.

While journalists have continually objected to the constraints they work under, there has been no concerted media effort to bypass, modify or overthrow the system of information control. Quiescence can be explained by the catch-22 of their position: renegades who actively seek to dissociate themselves from the government information system jeopardise their access to information; in Britain this can make their job virtually undoable unless they are willing to join the ranks of the marginalised, radical press.

What is more difficult to justify is journalists' voluntary collusion with government sources and the way this collusion is kept hidden from consumers of their information. At every opportunity, examples of adversarial media–state relations are touted in the press while everyday participation in the parliamentary lobby and D-notice systems, and the use of officially and commercially produced sources of information is downplayed.[5] Collusion on a daily basis is not perhaps newsworthy, but the innate newsworthiness of detailed accounts of libel trials, contempt of court proceeding and disputes within the BBC over management, for example, which straw polls suggest are read by few and understood by fewer still, is never questioned, perhaps because such coverage buttresses the adversarial model.

The foundations of information control

The OSA was underpinned – and, paradoxically, simultaneously undermined – by a variety of bureaucratic arrangements instituted to facilitate the continued dissemination of official information in spite of the constraints imposed by the new law. The parliamentary lobby, in which accredited journalists are allowed into the lobby of Westminster to receive briefings from 'unattributable' official sources, was founded in 1884; its creation coincided with the arrival of mass democracy and reflected early state attempts to defuse democratic power by controlling not only official information but also political reporting.

The lobby is intuitively regarded as a 'bad thing' because of the compromises it forces on journalists, but attempts to undermine its legitimacy through nonparticipation are scarce. In 1963 opposition leader Harold Wilson launched a stinging attack on the practice of unattributable Foreign Office briefings:

Nothing is said to Parliament by the Foreign Office, and diplomatic correspondents are reduced to utter dependence on a daily briefing ... If the press exercises its right to criticise, then facilities dry up. Correspondents are demoted from the inner ring to the outer ring, and are denied information altogether in a system of administrative blackballing.[6]

The *Sunday Times*, buoyed by this attack, appointed Anthony Howard to be a non-lobby Whitehall correspondent the following year when Wilson was elected Prime Minister. The Wilson government, however, forbade civil servants to speak to Howard and imposed strict conditions under which ministers could speak to him. Other newspapers were unsupportive and within eight months the experiment was abandoned, Howard's position outside the magic ring of the information-rich lobby having become untenable.[7]

Having apparently decided that the lobby cannot be beaten, it is now simply joined, its legitimacy such that opposition parties no longer criticise it but ape this state-sanctioned propaganda machine by running shadow lobbies. The excuse offered – with some justification – is that information that might otherwise never emerge is divulged under these circumstances. However, as long as the press voluntarily continues to support the lobby, less compromised methods of gaining information are unlikely to emerge.

D-notices are the other side of the lobby coin; in the lobby, journalists are told what they can print, while D-notices advise them on what they cannot print. The D-notice system was set up in 1912 to guide newspapers on officially proscribed areas, usually involving issues of national and military security, a function it still fulfils. D-notices are issued by a nominally independent committee made up of civil servants and journalists who consult on what restrictions should apply.

The D-notice system is unique in that the media participate in it voluntarily, an aspect that serves the state's purposes because, as Harry Street points out, 'much less odium attaches to an arrangement to which press and broadcasting authorities are freely consenting and participating parties'.[8] Another unique feature is that it is the media that fund the D-notice system: the Newspaper Proprietors' Association pays the salaries and operating costs of the committee. For 40 years the press refused to admit that it participated in drawing up and paying for its own censorship. David Hooper points out that such a arrangement would not even be considered *legal* in the United States.[9]

Reliance on commercially and/or officially produced information is also deemed to be very important – and destructive – to British newspaper culture. With limited resources and an absence of alternative sources of information, the media have become overreliant on 'ready-made' material, especially where political and media interests coincide. In the 1992 election campaign, the pro-Conservative *Sunday Express* ran stories about Labour and Liberal Democrat candidates based on dossiers produced by the Conservative Central Office.[10] These dossiers emphasised such 'socialist' activities as visiting Eastern Bloc countries and the refusal of one Labour candidate to attend a Buckingham Palace garden party. The dossier on Liberal Democratic leader Paddy Ashdown included five pages of quotations intended to raise doubts about Ashdown's suitability for political office, including such confessions as 'The last act each day is a whisky and a cigarette' and 'I'm a terrible driver.'[11]

Recent studies suggest that outside sources of information continue to diminish in quality, although not necessarily in quantity, as journalism becomes increasingly industrialised. In addition to government constraints on information, there are the sheer physical constraints imposed by the changing demands of the job itself. Compared to the 1960s and 1970s, journalists working on national newspapers are now heavily concentrated in London; their number has remained about the same as compared to the 1960s, but there are more newspapers and newspapers are twice as big, requiring journalists to work, it is estimated, three times as hard. In such a context,

> It is hardly surprising that their world has been reduced, or that a few global media empires are forming self-enclosed, self-reinforcing systems in which the reality defined or invented by one arm of the system is validated by the others. In such systems there is no external reference point from which to take your moral bearings.[12]

The extent to which journalists, newspaper proprietors and policy-makers share the same political world view and how this condominium of interests effects media outputs is difficult to assess. The consequences of the establishment of formal bureaucratic control over the dissemination of official information is somewhat more concrete. Specific empirical data on the OSA can be used to suggest ways in which the adversarial model of media–state relations does not map onto reality. Official secrecy cases have been reported selectively in the press in ways that enhance liberal claims about how the media operate in the British state. The empirical record suggests the use of the OSA *against* the media differs greatly from how it has been portrayed *by* the media. Not only are there surprisingly few prosecutions of the press – and only the word 'press' applies, as the broadcast media have never been formally charged with OSA violations – but those that have occurred do not bear out the picture of courageous journalists fighting against government repression and safeguarding democracy. Media prosecutions have not involved reporters uncovering Watergate-sized scandals, but rather have entailed reporters grubbing around in the lowest echelons of the civil service for murderers' confessions, celebrity gossip and crime stories. With rare exceptions, there is little suggestion of investigative political journalism being hampered by the OSA, and, where such exceptions occur, the media establishment has been reluctant to support the temerity of individual journalists.

The media fixation on the OSA as an instrument of government repression has affected the way OSA trials are covered. The mere threat of OSA-backed censorship invariably receives a great deal of publicity, and certain prosecutions against newspapers or reporters have become *causes célèbres*, serving ever after as examples of the healthily adversarial model of media–state relations. Other examples that show the press in a less favourable light have faded into obscurity.

Suppressing the press, 1911–1952

Press–state relations are indeed adversarial sometimes, and this tension occasionally manifested itself in early battles over government attempts to move official secrecy onto a bureaucratic footing. Journalists rightly feared that the OSA would be used to limit freedom of the press and were prepared to resist. It was policy-makers' fear of press resistance that led to journalists not being targeted by the 1889 OSA and to the delay of the introduction of the 1911 OSA until a convincing national security threat presented itself. However, once in place, the OSA was used almost exclusively to deter leaks and to extend government information control into situations in which national security did not obtain. Between 1911 and 1952, only eleven OSA cases were brought that directly involved the press; none of these had a national security element, or even much political content.

In 1920, in an attempt to extend wartime practices into peacetime, the government introduced amendments to the OSA which were again fiercely resisted by the media. A main source of contention lay in the proposed new section 6, which would give the state powers to force individuals to supply information to the police in the event of suspected OSA violations. The press felt the new powers would be used to force reporters to reveal sources. Attorney General Sir Gordon Hewitt scoffed, 'it is said that this Bill deals with the Press. That seems to me an astonishing statement.'[13] In an articulation of policy-makers's continued attempts to create legally defined but content-vague categories of patriotism and disloyalty, he argued that

> we are dealing with spying and attempts at spying ... It is the moral duty already of every good citizen, if he has information about spying or attempted spying, to communicate that information to the authorities ... I cannot think that it can be regarded as harsh that the Bill should make a statutory duty of that which is already a moral duty.[14]

This position forced the media onto the defensive since any protest they mounted could be suggestive of their dereliction of moral duty in safeguarding the state. Section 6 was passed and used on a number of occasions to force newspapers to disclose sources before its scope was narrowed in 1939 to allow interrogation powers only in suspected espionage cases, 'the only occasion on which Parliament has backpedalled in official secrets legislation', David Williams notes.[15]

In 1930, an early example of what appeared to be investigative journalism was revealed as official incompetence when the government unsuccessfully invoked section 6 to force reporters to disclose sources following the publication of stories about the imminent arrest of Gandhi.[16] A furious government called for an investigation into the source of the leak; Special Branch interrogated one reporter for five hours under the powers of section 6. What their interrogation uncovered was that the leak had come from a Parliamentary Private Secretary and corroborated by none other than the Home Secretary. The investigation was quickly dropped and, in the wake of the furore, the Attorney General offered assurances that no action against reporters under section 6 would be undertaken without his express consent, thereby ensuring that section 6 would not be abused at lower levels of authority.

Despite such assurances, the state continued to pursue cases. In 1937 the police impelled the Manchester *Daily Dispatch* to reveal the source of a description of a fraud suspect. The description had been gleaned from a police circular which, although widely available and not marked 'confidential', was in fact found to be confidential. The defence launched an appeal based on whether police information was even covered by section 2. The court affirmed that police were Crown servants, thereby opening the OSA up to include a whole new range of public servants. The appeal was heard by the now Lord Chancellor Justice Hewitt – the minister who had assured Parliament in 1920 that the OSA applied only to spies.[17]

The press and the state during the Cold War

Media–state relations changed with the onset of the Cold War. If the state hoped to incorporate the citizenry into defeating the Soviet menace, the press would play a central role in defining attitudes. The state had to relinquish its monopoly on national security affairs and delegate some trust to the media. James Margach remarks that 'the need to hold together the Western alliance, and to keep their public's support for a tough policy, led the Governments of Britain and the United States to go to un-usual lengths to play their cards face upwards'.[18] Mutual coopera-tion rather than conflict meant that the media were given greater access to information and, as a kind of quid pro quo, press prosecutions virtually ceased after 1950 in spite of a plethora of government-rocking security scandals. Ordinary muckraking no longer resulted in charges being laid.

This may have been a more responsible usage of the OSA on the part of the state, but the historical record equally suggests the paucity of the journalistic community's attempts to provoke a genuine debate about Cold War security and, in particular, Brit-ain's participation in the balance of terror. From the late 1950s, journalists working in the forbidden zone of national security on behalf of the public interest were shown little quarter by the courts, the state or their media colleagues. It was only that whistleblowers actually occupied the moral highground that thwarted state at-tempts to gain convictions in cases where government wrongdoing was exposed. In such cases, it was the jury that was often the saviour.

The general timidity of the media contrasted with the sea change taking place in public attitudes. With postwar governments increasingly involved in all aspects of the community, from economic intervention to education and health, the electorate was growing more assertive in response, not only demanding govern-ment action in ever-broadening fields but also demanding greater accountability. Calls for open government and freedom of informa-tion were heard increasingly, and senior politicians and adminis-trators concurred that reforms to the operation of Whitehall and to the dissemination of official information were necessary.

On the face of things, both media and state were openly committed to dismantling the secret state, but the pursuit of security had to be balanced against its political costs, no small problem in a quickly liberalising and assertively democratic society with rising political expectations. In 1968 the Fulton Committee, convened to examine reform of the civil service, recommended that 'the government should set up an enquiry to make recommendations for getting rid of unnecessary secrecy in this country. Clearly the Official Secrets Act would need to be included in this review.'[19]

The rising popular demand for less secrecy was echoed by both the Conservative and Labour parties. In 1969 Edward Heath called for a reform of the OSA and contempt and libel laws, noting that

> What was once a law specifically framed to counter espionage has in too many cases been used to hide facts and figures that may be inconvenient or embarrassing to the government of the day, but which, strictly speaking, are not secrets at all.[20]

Weeks later, Harold Wilson announced that the government was considering revamping the OSA in accordance with the Fulton recommendations to ensure that government's 'duty to preserve the security of the state is not used as an excuse to restrict the freedom of the press'.[21] Despite the rhetoric, a mere week later an attempt to pass a Private Member's Freedom of Publication (Protection) Bill, proposing amendments to official secrecy, libel and contempt laws, came under such a ferocious government attack that Michael Foot remarked 'one could see the marks of blood on the floor'.[22]

The mainstream media were unwilling to spearhead change. Instead, they assisted the state in creating a national consensus about the new national security agenda, becoming a conduit – both witting and unwitting – for government disinformation designed to engineer public support. Chapman Pincher admitted that in 1957 he had cooperated with the Ministry of Defence in planting a false story in his newspaper to diffuse opposition to hydrogen bomb tests planned at Christmas Island. Journalists invited to witness the second test filed their stories before the test even took place to avoid being scooped by rival newspapers. Although the tests were flops, they were reported as huge successes.[23] While such anecdotes cannot do more than suggest the depth of media support of the Cold War security agenda, it seems apparent from the prosecution record at least that the media tended to support rather than challenge the status quo.

The real catalyst for change to the OSA came not from a general commitment to reform but from the simple failure of the OSA to serve the purpose it had done so admirably in a more deferential political climate. In 1971 the *Sunday Telegraph* was acquitted for publishing a confidential government report in a case that made a mockery of the whole prosecution process. Another debacle occurred in 1977 when the state only just managed to make reduced charges stick to maverick journalist Duncan Campbell. If the OSA could no longer be relied upon to ensure reporters' discretion, then the state would have to find other means, which it did. Contempt and libel laws and injunctions proved surprisingly effective at cowing journalists and had the advantage of muddying the democratic pitch. Contempt and libel were more difficult legal concepts to package attractively for the punters and consequently less controversial than the black and white issues presented by use and abuse of the OSA.

The Sunday Telegraph case, 1971

The 1971 *Sunday Telegraph* case centred on a political row over the leak of a confidential report about the Nigerian civil war. It was a wonderful occasion for the media to present themselves in a favourable light and newspaper elites practically begged to be included on the charge sheets; whatever the outcome of the case, the defendants were assured of scoring a resounding moral victory. The court proceedings were turned into a show trial, designed to sport media courage in the face of repression, a representation of secrecy that once again served the purposes of the elites. The real issue in democratic terms concerned the government's misleading of parliament; this aspect was lost in the raucous debate over so-called press freedom.

But even here courage was lacking. The journalist charged, Jonathan Aitken, and the newspaper that ran his story would have accepted the state's quiet offer to have them plead guilty in a magistrate's court and receive small fines. It was Colonel Douglas Cairns who contested the section 2 charge, thereby forcing the case into a Crown court. Cairns, a retired soldier seconded to the British observation team in Nigeria, committed the initial leak. As a matter of course, he sent a confidential report to Major-General Henry Templer Alexander, his former superior in the observation team who liked to be kept abreast of events. The report dealt with the civil war between federal Nigerian forces and the breakaway Biafran forces and discussed how the British government was secretly supporting the federal troops materially – the government was significantly understating publicly the amount of aid being given. The report also alleged corruption and inefficiency in the Nigerian high command. Potentially politically embarrassing, it was marked 'confidential'; the court would be told that its author had remarked such a designation would ensure a wide distribution in diplomatic circles. Furthermore, a Foreign Office official defined for the court what was meant by 'confidential':

> a government official who thought that the disclosure of a document might cause embarrassment to Her Majesty's Government might well classify it as confidential. Naturally, I mean politically embarrassing ... Embarrassment and security are not really two different things.[24]

Attempting to score a debating point over after-dinner port, Alexander, a supporter of the federal side, gave the report to Aitken, a supporter of Biafran independence. Aitken realised the report was potential political dynamite and supplied copies to other members of the pro-Biafran lobby, including Hugh Fraser MP, Yorkshire Television and the *Sunday Telegraph*. The *Sunday Telegraph* had it cleared by the D-notice Committee, which found that since the report dealt with non-UK forces, its publication would not fall under the British security remit covered by D-notices. It was, however, an official document and therefore covered by the OSA, a point the secretary of the D-notice Committee claimed to have made clear to the paper.[25] The assistant editor later said that not only had the OSA never been mentioned in the conversation, but that it had never occurred to him that they might be committing a violation – an interesting comment on the OSA's reputed chilling effect on the media.[26] The paper also ignored two informal warnings from friendly Foreign Office officials.

The report was published, but its impact was diminished by the sudden defeat of the Biafran forces. With the potential for a breach of security defused, the only issue left facing the government was whether it could tolerate such a blatant violation of its information monopoly. It opted to proceed with the case, but the problem of simultaneously muzzling and protecting members of the elites pushed the prosecution team into untenable contortions. Cairns was charged with leaking the document to Alexander, but

Alexander was not charged with receiving it, nor for passing it on to Aitken; instead, he appeared as the star prosecution witness. Aitken was charged for leaking the document to several sources. Hugh Fraser and Lord Hartwell, the proprietor of the paper, were not prosecuted, although both acknowledged publicly that they had committed offences.

The defence established during the committal proceedings that almost all the supposedly confidential information contained in the report had already been published elsewhere. The prosecution set about building its case on the commission of a technical breach of section 2.[27] The question of guilt hinged on *mens rea* and, without Alexander standing in the dock, it was difficult to establish the necessary chain of guilty knowledge. Justice Cauldfield warned Alexander not to incriminate himself as he took the stand and then ordered the jury to acquit the trio, making a scathing attack on section 2 from the bench.

The embarrassing failure to secure a conviction for this clear offence was enough to warn the state off using the OSA again unless it was in circumstances in which it was likely to win. In 1972 the police began investigating the leak of a confidential Department of the Environment policy review document to the *Railway Gazette* concerning a plan to close down a third of the rail network. The *Gazette* story was picked up by the *Sunday Times*. Allegations emerged that the police raided the *Gazette* offices, tapped phones, threatened to reveal a sexually embarrassing phone call in order to find out who had leaked the document, and then interrogated the *Sunday Times* editor. No charges were laid, although whether as a direct result of the *Sunday Telegraph* debacle or through worry about the police treatment of journalists is not clear. Charges were again withdrawn in 1974 in a case brought against two researchers for *Time Out* magazine who were arrested for unlawful possession of a Ministry of Defence manual, *Counter-Revolutionary Operations*, after a picture of the manual appeared in *Time Out*. The picture had already appeared in an Irish newspaper.

A number of embarrassing high-level leaks occurred in 1975–76, but the temptation to use the OSA was still resisted. To quash publication of former cabinet minister Richard Crossman's diaries, the Attorney General sought a High Court injunction to prevent publication on the grounds that the principle of cabinet responsibility would be undermined. Another storm broke in June 1976 when cabinet minutes outlining the government's U-turn on its child benefit scheme were leaked to the magazine

New Statesman. The use of the OSA to justify the subsequent attempts to identify the leak was opposed by opposition leader Margaret Thatcher, who said it should only be used to protect national security, 'not the security of ministers and civil servants from the consequences of their own mistakes'.[28]

The ABC case, 1977

The most serious battle between the press and the state occurred in 1977 when two journalists and their source were charged with espionage. It is an extremely rare example of genuine investigative journalism into the secret state and an excellent example of how far the state was willing to go to quash such investigations. The three were not simply charged with unauthorised disclosure; the espionage charge elevated their offence to a felony. The prosecution argued that, by investigating the activities of the security and intelligence services, the defendants were threatening British national security. The defence's case rested on proving that 'national security' was once again being used to cloak legitimate inquiries into possibly illegitimate state activities.

Duncan Campbell, a freelance journalist specialising in national security, had already earned the opprobrium of the security state for his work on a 1976 article entitled 'The Eavesdroppers', a detailed account of GCHQ and its relationship with the American National Security Agency. The article was co-written by American reporter Mark Hosenball and assisted by renegade ex-CIA agent Phillip Agee who had previously made disclosures that may have led to the murder of a CIA operative. Agee's associations with radical British journalists worried both American and British authorities. GCHQ wanted Campbell prosecuted but lacked evidence, indicative of the state's reluctance to embark upon another difficult OSA case. The authorities instead deported Hosenball and Agee on national security grounds. A defence committee set up to protest the deportations and loosely associated with the National Council of Civil Liberties was then subjected to security service harassment, its members suffering a series of break-ins, thefts, phone taps, surveillance and mail openings.

John Berry, a former member of the Signals Intelligence (Sigint) Corps, contacted the defence committee and met with two of its members, Campbell and another journalist, Crispin Aubrey. Berry spent three hours describing his Sigint work to

Campbell, who taped the conversation. Aubrey, finding the technical nature of the discussion over his head, was bored by the meeting. When the gathering broke up, all three were arrested by Special Branch officers, held incommunicado for 42 hours, then charged, initially under section 2. Bail was refused and they were remanded in a top-security wing of Brixton Prison under precautions usually reserved for terrorists. Later, Aubrey and Campbell were granted restricted bail. Special Branch raided Campbell's flat and found hundreds of photographs, slides and notes on the British defence establishment, radar systems and communications networks.

Seven weeks after their arrests, an espionage charge was added to the section 2 charges and the prosecution attempted to mount a national security show trial, introducing unnamed witnesses, *in camera* proceedings and extensive jury vetting to justify the astonishing decision to charge the three with espionage. Claiming the sensitivity of the Sigint-related evidence required special precautions: 82 jurors were vetted. The twelve chosen – the defence's objections to the jury composition were overruled – included an ex-SAS officer as foreman, an ex-squadron security clerk and a civil servant, all signatories of the OSA. Just before the tape of Berry's Sigint revelations was about to be played to a closed court, the jury sent a note to the judge explaining that some of the jurors feared breaching the OSA by listening to it.

The prosecutor opened the committal proceedings by outlining the security implications of the disclosures and particularly the danger posed by Campbell: 'It is not suggested that he was in the employ of a foreign power, but he was thoroughly subversive.'[29] After playing the Sigint tape, the prosecution produced its expert witness, identified only as 'Colonel B' to safeguard his identity. The prosecution had withdrawn its preferred witness – whose identity was 'too secret' even to be revealed to the trial judge – when the court refused to guarantee his anonymity to the extent demanded by the prosecution.

The secrecy surrounding Colonel B became a linchpin for action in the radical press when two fringe leftwing newspapers published his name and position – Colonel Hugh Johnstone, former head of Sigint. The National Union of Journalists (NUJ) journal followed suit, and soon a plethora of contempt proceedings was under way.[30] At the same time, the annual NUJ conference began in Whitley Bay and the gathering was warned by the Director of Public Prosecutions (DPP) that any mention of Johnstone's name would result in high court action. The forbidden name was carved in the Whitley Bay sands and hung from banners outside the conference, but inside the NUJ buckled to official pressure and refused to debate motions that named Johnstone. Bernard Levin argued the establishment press's point of view at the conference: 'we do not believe that those who face spurious martyrdom should have their halo paid for through members' subscriptions'.[31]

There was less reticence in the Commons, where four Labour MPs, protected by parliamentary privilege, uttered the *verboten* name. Television and radio broadcasts duly reported it and the DPP sent out further warnings about contempt proceedings. It was with this attempt to muzzle parliament that the government over-stepped the mark. Even the normally staid *Times* published Johnstone's name, explaining 'we consider it our overriding duty to continue providing full, fair and faithful reporting of Parliamen-tary proceedings as we have been doing for nearly two hundred years'.[32]

Support for Aubrey, Berry and Campbell, the three defend-ants in what had become known as the ABC case, was concen-trated at the margins of the system, in the radical press and in the safety of parliament. The mainstream media only climbed on board when the government grossly overstepped its authority. While it was generally held that prosecuting the journalists for espionage was going too far, the reluctance to back Campbell in particular is indicative of the innate conservatism of the media in national security matters.

Ironically, this tepid support took place against a backdrop of deliberation over the future of the OSA. Campbell actually based his not guilty plea on Home Secretary Merlyn Rees's 1976 decla-ration that 'The Government accepts that the mere receipt of official information should no longer be an offence.'[33] As to the Sigint involvement, during the course of the hearings the defence produced legally published material that even the prosecution admitted was more damaging to security than anything Campbell had acquired from Berry. The first trial collapsed over a scandal over jury vetting; the second trial judge threw out the espionage charges, recommending that section 1 be restricted to spying.

Left to prove the commission of a section 2 offence, the prosecu-tion would have had a relatively easy time but for the political problem caused by Rees's announcement. The prosecution tried to argue that Campbell had not simply 'received' information but had instigated the offence. Even on these lesser charges, the jury agon-ised and only returned a verdict when threatened with dismissal. Berry's case proved the most straightforward: Justice Mars-Jones directed the jury to find Berry guilty, noting that whether Berry's information was secret or not was immaterial. Berry argued that he felt he had a moral duty to make his disclosures; Mars-Jones claimed the acceptance of such a defence would make a mockery of protective practices against disclosure. 'We will not tolerate defectors or whistleblowers from our services who seek the assistance of the press or other media to publicize secrets, whatever the motive', he said. 'In future they will go to prison.'[34] Berry received a two-year suspended sentence, its leniency reflecting the oppressive conditions he had lived under for the previous 20 months. Campbell and Aubrey were also found guilty but received conditional discharges and were ordered to pay £5000 towards prosecution costs. The outcome of the trial suggests that Aubrey and Campbell had had a narrow escape – the judge hearing the first trial claimed he would have jailed them.

Journalists like Campbell posed a difficult problem for the state as well as for the media. Hooper writes that 'the government apparently failed to understand what Campbell was doing and how he collected his information – not by subverting soldiers but by avidly collecting published material on defence'.[35] His efforts to investigate and expose illegitimate activities carried out by the state under the cloak of 'national security' alarmed the security and intelligence services, who provided guidance and support to the prosecution. The state feared that one day Campbell – or someone like him – might open up a Pandora's box of genuine state secrets and publicise them. A clear message needed to be sent to the population, reminding them that they were unfit to know and judge the effects of their actions. The contrary suggestion that citizens should have the right to question the activities of the secret state was moot.

The mainstream media largely followed the state's position, agreeing that Campbell's activities were not something they could support. Aubrey and Campbell operated on the fringes of journalism, working as freelances and campaigners with specific political agendas. Their marginality earned them little sympathy, although here was an apparently just cause for journalists. The media were largely willing to accept that maverick journalists should be treated like suspected terrorists and punished as spies. The media's willingness to accede to espionage charges being appropriate is a disturbing comment on media–state relations.

In a sense, both sides won in the ABC case. A technical breach had been committed and was punished: the Crown had its conviction. The reduced charges and light sentences were a judi-

cial chastisement to the state, which in equating legitimate journalistic enquiry with espionage had attempted to push the scope
of the OSA too far. Resistance to state censorship in this case
came from individuals within the judiciary, parliament and on
the margins of journalism. Mainstream behaviour suggested a
depth of support for the state's maintenance of its secretive
stance on national security issues.

The Sarah Tisdall case, 1984

The *Guardian*'s 1984 sellout of Sarah Tisdall stands as another
example of how the mainstream press, whether it supports the
left or the right, ultimately supports the establishment and is
only willing to challenge the state within certain narrow parameters.[36] In 1983 Tisdall, a junior clerk in the Foreign Office,
leaked two documents to the *Guardian* concerning the scheduled
arrival of cruise missiles at Greenham Common. One document
formed the basis of a front page story the following day, although
the second was judged to be too sensitive to use. While willing to
exploit some of the material for his scoop, *Guardian* editor Peter
Preston was unwilling to protect his source: he turned over documentation to the authorities that led to the conviction of Tisdall.
She received a six-month sentence for unauthorised disclosure;
Preston, who could have been charged for receipt and unauthorised disclosure, was not.

Although the *Guardian* challenged the Crown's right to
demand the return of the documents, the decision to return them
distressed at least some of the journalistic community, which felt
that Preston had an ethical – if not a legal – right to protect
Tisdall by refusing to provide the Crown with the evidence it
needed to incriminate her. This may have invited a contempt of
court charge, but the protection of sources, even by 'illegal'
means, is generally vindicated. Certainly public and press sympathies seldom lie with the government in such cases; it is widely
accepted that newspapers should fight to protect sources and the
NUJ voted overwhelmingly to condemn Preston and the *Guardian* for giving in. Aidan White, the NUJ's secretary-treasurer
(and a *Guardian* sub-editor), explained: 'Journalists should go to
jail, not sources.'[37] The criticism of Preston's action might have
been derived from the impression that, by failing to protect
Tisdall, the *Guardian* was undermining the liberal fiction of a
courageous press standing up against the government.

The right to protect sources is guaranteed under section 10 of the Contempt of Court Act 1981, which says that unless the state can show that protection jeopardises national security, justice and the prevention of crime and/or disorder, refusing to disclose sources is acceptable.[38] The *Guardian*'s appeal was, in the words of the *Guardian*'s QC, a test of whether section 10 'does give real protection against compulsion to disclose sources' and not merely 'nominal protection to be easily defeated by the untested evidence of an official who simply says that disclosure of a source is necessary in the national interest' – a question perhaps of only academic interest to Tisdall, who was well into her sentence when the appeal was finally resolved.[39] The *Guardian* lost the appeal by three votes to two; this outcome was ascribed to the rather unfortunate composition of the panel hearing the case: which included two former chairs of the Security Commission predisposed to take a wide view of what jeopardises national security. One of the dissenting judges, Lord Scarman, felt that the evidence 'fell far short' of that needed to prove that disclosure was in the interests of national security.[40]

The OSA was reformed in 1989, but the narrowing of its ambit did not result in any noticeable improvement in political journalism. Information concerning the Matrix-Churchill affair, the BCCI scandal, the Maxwell pensions fraud and the exposure of accounting irregularities in the Property Services Agency and the Legal Aid Board was not dug up by journalists but came through whistleblowers and government agencies such as the National Audit Office and Customs and Excise.[41] This situation is likely to obtain as long as the lobby remains intact, D-notices are adhered to and the press relies on prepared information rather than investigative journalism.

British official secrecy is not simply 'produced' by British policy-makers at the centre of the state who are trying to keep the rest of the world at bay and in ignorance; although journalists are left to function as best they can within the parameters they are given, their complicity in the state's information regime simply perpetuates the excessive amount of secrecy in Britain and the project of silencing alternative discourses. The media endeavour to legitimate their increasingly powerful role by constantly emphasising their contributions to democratic principles, relying on the spurious mythology of the liberty of the press. Although in practice few journalists have been punished under its terms, the OSA plays a major role in this fictitious battle between liberty and authority, standing as 'proof' of the media's efforts to safeguard democracy by fighting for press freedom. Yet the evidence suggests that the rhetoric afforded by a handful of cases obscures the realities of collusion and compromise which the British media operate under. As long as the media continue to support a system that compromises them while publicly maintaining their independence and their centrality to the operation of British democracy, this system will endure.

CHAPTER 6

RESISTANCE AND REFORM UNDER THATCHER

Whilst not as open as the United States of America or Germany, the United Kingdom has avoided the horrors of the Soviet Union or Sadaam Hussein's Iraq.

Richard Thurlow, historian [1]

The Thatcher revolution

Hounded by the press, in 1979 new Prime Minister Margaret Thatcher admitted to parliament that in 1964 MI5 made an immunity deal with Anthony Blunt. Blunt was a member of the Cambridge Comintern, the coterie of Soviet master spies that had been spawned within the British elite itself. Third cousin of the Queen Mother, distinguished art professor, Cambridge fellow, Knight Commander of the Royal Victorian Order and consort of Buckingham palace, Blunt had enjoyed nearly two decades of life at the very centre of the British establishment even after he had been secretly unmasked as a Soviet mole, testament to the willingness of the elites to cover up treachery within their own ranks. Thatcher, a grocer's daughter, a woman, was an outsider. Although her admission of Blunt's secret history and MI5's deal was forced, not volunteered, it did prove to be a harbinger of things to come. Under Thatcher, the status quo would change.

What was different about the Thatcher government was its unusual willingness to use legal-rational means to try to seize control of the disparate powers sited at the centre of the state. In her efforts to change how the British state worked, Thatcher challenged powerful vested interests at the political centre – within the civil service, the security and intelligence services and the press – and often they rebelled.

The paradox of Thatcher's era was that, while on the one hand the legal-rational state became more centralised and de-democratised, in response, resistance became more powerful and effective. Through whistleblowing, resistors moved outside the boundaries of the legal-rational state to appeal directly to the population and were thus able to provide some check on the excesses of Thatcher's power. The state's predictable response was to close off the loopholes that whistleblowers were exploiting in attempts to dam the flow of democratic power that such resistance represented.

In 1979, the 'secret state' was still the lacuna at the heart of British governance; the 1970s impetus for reform – demands for freedom of information, freedom of the press, increased accountability and transparency – faded with the election of a Conservative government. The polity itself seemed compliant. The historian Bernard Porter notes that Britons were more spied upon in the 1970s and 1980s than perhaps they had been in their entire history, but public opposition to state intrusion had all but melted away.[2] It was against this background of apparent quiescence that radical changes were made. By 1993, the security and intelligence services were on a legal footing, the OSA had been replaced and such was the new policy of openness that MI5 head Stella Rimington appeared publicly to lecture journalists on the role of the security services. In the history of the secret state, this was nothing less than a revolution. The irony was that it was the Thatcher government, notorious for its disregard of civil liberties, misuse of the security and intelligence services, abuse of police powers, politicisation of the bureaucracy, censorship of the media, and generally authoritarian style of governing, that delivered to the polity an unprecedented view into the darkest reaches of British governance.

Repressive power relations carry the seeds of resistance and empowerment: repression makes resistance possible because it can be a catalyst for consciousness-raising and politicisation. Foucault took the rigid repression of sexuality during the Victorian era as one example.[3] The classification of specific types of sexual behaviour as deviant contributed to the development of 'reverse discourse' among the deviant groups: 'homosexuality began to speak in its own behalf ... using the same categories by which it was medically disqualified'.[4] Political scientists can find an analogy in debates on state responses to terrorism, where repressive measures can create sympathy for and identification with the perpetrators of terrorist violence.

The relationship between repression and resistance manifested itself publicly in the British state when the Thatcher government imposed increasingly politically charged security policies on the population. As individuals and groups within the demos felt the mantle of state repression fall upon them, their individual experiences began to gel into a genuine, if disparate, opposition to the state's abuse of power. The difference between this resistance and resistance mounted under previous governments, however, was the target of the repression. Thatcher's programmes stirred up dissent at the centre of the state within powerful groups like Whitehall, the security and intelligence services and the media. While such groups were willing to accept some changes to the contemporary political landscape, they drew the line when their own interests were too fundamentally challenged, and, unlike the 'average' citizen, such groups wielded sufficient power to resist successfully. It was this resistance at the centre that led to growing public awareness of how the secret state operated. As the ensuing frays spilled out into the public domain, the contours of the amorphous and mysterious 'secret state' began to crystallise into something that was both discrete from and integral to the practice of democracy in Britain. With such knowledge came a degree of empowerment.

The extent to which the national political consciousness had been raised is particularly obvious in the cultural sphere. In the early 1980s a spate of television serials, documentaries and films explored and popularised the secret side of British political power. The producer of the film *Defence of the Realm* said that, when the script was first mooted in 1980, the story was considered a paranoid, leftwing conspiracy theory fantasy. By the time of its release in the mid-1980s, the possibility existed that the sinister world it depicted might have more basis in reality than people imagined. Through the 1980s, as the electorate witnessed the *Spycatcher* allegations, the controversy surrounding John Stalker's investigation of a shoot-to-kill policy in Northern Ireland, Cathy Massiter's revelations about MI5 surveillance, and rumours about MI5 plots to drive Harold Wilson from power, such films began to seem prophetic rather than paranoid.

The security and intelligence services

In 1979, official attitudes to the security and intelligence services differed little from their nineteenth-century forebears' propensity to view spying as a necessary evil, the less said about the better, although latterly this ostrich-like approach was born of political pragmatism, not Victorian sensibilities. There was a great deal to be said in favour of continuing to pretend that MI5, MI6 and GCHQ did not exist. No electoral capital could be gained in trying to bring the security and intelligence services to heel, and public debate would almost certainly lead to revelations about past dirty tricks, stir up concerns about civil liberties and provoke demands for reforms that would not only curtail the centre's power but rile the powerful vested interests of the security and intelligence services. Furthermore, such moves might antagonise the delicate web of security and defence relationships conjoining Britain to its anticommunist allies. Finally – and perhaps worst of all – genuine accountability would implicate the government when things went wrong. Denial of knowledge of activities and operations was – and remains – a Minister's best defence.

Although divisions between governments and the security and intelligence services sometimes ran deep, disagreements were kept out of the public eye; however problematic the secret services might be, the alternative of democratic oversight promised to be worse. While there had been periodic demands for reform and numerous election pledges to undertake the task of undoing the excessive amount of secrecy in the British state, once in power, governments invariably hesitated. Thatcher's predecessor, Prime Minister James Callaghan, in an abnegation of official responsibility not at all atypical of policy-makers, suggested that the best way to deal with the secret services was simply to trust them:

> I am certain there must be a very high degree of responsibility among those who serve in MI5 or MI6 because they have very great powers, considerable powers, and I think the ethos of those services is as important as the degrees of accountability that can visit upon them.[5]

Callaghan may have been correct in his belief that service ethos was important, but morale was low following the turmoil of the 1960s and 1970s. The hunt for the 'ultimate' Soviet mole within MI5 spawned paranoia and suspicion rather than *esprit de corps*, even as the state's need for the secret services was growing. On the one hand, the intensification of the Troubles in Northern Ireland and the extension of the IRA campaign onto the British mainland in the 1970s led to tightening internal security and the introduction of new laws such as the Prevention of Terrorism Act. On the other hand, the centre's traditional suspicion of the left was expanding. The miners' strikes of the early 1970s, and, later, the 'Winter of Discontent' that caused Callaghan's downfall, seemed to underscore the restiveness and danger inhering in the British masses. In response, political surveillance was stepped up throughout the 1970s to encompass peace activists, trade unionists, people who wrote critical letters to newspapers and other groups that fell under the rubric of what was referred to internally as the 'far and wide left'.[6] So extreme was the security service's view of what constituted threat that MI5 officer Miranda Ingram remarked that some officers 'thought that people who wore jeans were potentially subversive'.[7]

In contrast to Callaghan's studied ignorance, Thatcher took a close interest in the security and intelligence services and her 1980s reconfiguration of British internal security was partly a matter of design, partly inadvertent. While 'trust' in the security and intelligence services might have placated the public in the 1970s, decades of slow rot had left the secret state on shaky foundations; these crumbled under Thatcher's ambitious attempt to push MI5 in particular into controversial and increasingly partisan roles.

In foreign policy terms, national security was back on the agenda. With the onset of the second Cold War after a period of uneasy *détente*, Britain's Falklands adventure and continuing terrorism, the centre was provided with clear-cut threats, both external and internal, and policy-makers had sufficient justification for driving through difficult policies and quashing dissent. The OSA, so thoroughly discredited during the 1970s, underwent a renaissance, the number of prosecutions rivalling the security shake-ups of the 1960s when the state was found to be riddled with Soviet moles. But the OSA was just one indicator of the Thatcher government's efforts to increase the power of the centre *vis-à-vis* the demos. The 1980s began with moves to centralise police power and rewrite laws as the Thatcher government prepared to take on leftwing challenges like the trade unions and the antinuclear movement.

A major renovation that enabled the state to pin more subjects under its gaze was the widened definition of subversion. In 1963 Lord Denning had defined subversives as 'people who would contemplate the overthrow of government by unlawful means'.[8] In 1984–85 a new definition was officially adopted which removed the all-important proviso that activities be unlawful. The new definition included activities 'intended to undermine or overthrow parliamentary democracy by political, industrial or violent means', a retrograde step at a time when the concept of subversion was being reworked in other liberal democracies. Australia, finding the term too general, had replaced it with 'politically motivated violence' in 1986; in

New Zealand and Canadian law, people and groups engaged in 'lawful advocacy protest or dissent' were specifically protected from investigation by the security and intelligence services. But in Britain, the wide and woolly concept of national security was now joined by a wide and woolly working definition of subversion, and together these gave the centre the legal-rational justification for targeting political discourses antipathetic to the Thatcher programme. Trade union movements were outlawed and placed under surveillance, along with charities and citizens' groups.

The transformation of such apparently anodyne groups such as Shelter, the charity for the homeless, and Friends of the Earth, the environmental group, into threats to the British state was indicative of the Thatcher government's new spin on traditional elite prejudices towards an active citizenry exercising its legitimate political rights. Richard Thurlow has shown that official (and general) suspicion of the 'popular front' type of activities such as marches and demonstrations was by no means peculiar to the Thatcher government. In a political culture built on deference and civility, where dissent is tolerated only as long as it is contained within acceptable boundaries, popular resistance has never been popular – protest, if it is to occur, should occur at the ballot box rather than on the streets. Thurlow used the contemporary example of the official response to race relations problems to demonstrate the irony that this stance sometimes generates:

> Although the Race Relations Acts have been used against the instigators of racist behaviour aimed at immigrant groups, it remains true that more arrests have been made against those who protest against racial violence than those who either foment it or who were directly responsible for it.[9]

Actions taken against civil attempts at empowerment were therefore nothing new, but Thatcher's reorganisation and re-writing of the policing activities of the state shifted more power to the centre. Early on, Thatcher's inner cabal targeted a number of 'subversive' groups, subversive in the sense that they threatened Tory policy. It was resistance to this partisan reworking of threat that led to the unprecedented amounts of whistleblowing by disaffected officials. For example, Thatcher's small group of influential policy-makers and advisers particularly feared a CND–Labour linkage on unilateral nuclear disarmament which might make things uncomfortable during an election campaign. In 1983 a counter-propaganda unit was set up in Michael Heseltine's Ministry of Defence to discredit the antinuclear movement. According to a Tory official who was involved with the unit, tactics included 'information, disinformation and on many occasions, character assassination'.[10]

As a part of the effort to undermine possible electoral threats such as these, the government asked MI5 to violate its own operational codes and directives in order to provide the Tories with information on targeted groups. It was through the fissures this opened up within MI5 that the news of the new crackdown against the left leaked out. The major whistleblower was MI5 case officer Cathy Massiter, who was specifically concerned about the new policies concerning phone taps. Massiter was told that warrants for phone taps on CND members would be met favourably, even though CND was not considered a subversive group according to MI5's own operational code. This 'difficulty' was solved by positing Soviet involvement in CND, including possible funding.

MI5's working definition of subversion was stretched to encompass guilt by association in order to pursue CND activists. In 1985, Thatcher herself retroactively articulated MI5's new operational definition when she told the House that, in addition to individuals who belonged to legally defined subversive groups, an individual who 'is, or has recently been, sympathetic to or associated with members or sympathisers of such organisations or groups, in such a way as to raise reasonable doubts about his reliability [or] ... is susceptible to pressure from such organisations or groups' was also included.[11] In 1983 future CND chair Joan Ruddock had an MI5 file opened on her after she was interviewed by a Soviet journalist who was, unbeknown to her, a KGB officer. Another file was opened on CND executive officer Cathy Ashton, justified on the grounds that she shared a house with a Communist Party member. Such readings of national security rules satisfied both Whitehall and MI5 top brass, but Massiter objected to this high-level willingness to rewrite threats to the state. Massiter eventually left MI5 to go public with her criticisms of the new MI5 practice of feeding information to Michael Heseltine's propaganda unit. She also revealed that National Council for Civil Liberties' (NCCL) members Harriet Harman and Patricia Hewitt had been under MI5 surveillance and NCCL itself classed as 'subversive'.

Middle-ranking MI5 officer Michael Bettaney, working in the Soviet counterespionage section, expressed his disaffection from the changing security service by turning to espionage.[12] During a horrific tour of duty in Northern Ireland, Bettaney, a Catholic, had developed doubts about British policy in Ireland. Like Massiter, he grew increasingly troubled about MI5 surveillance operations that targeted legitimate groups; he also worried about the state of crisis between East and West. He took a very different route from Massiter however, when he decided he should use his position in MI5 to help reduce the state of Cold War by becoming a Soviet spy.

Bettaney delivered an envelope containing information about the detection and expulsion of three Soviet intelligence officers to the KGB contact in London, but was rebuffed by the KGB, which suspected he was an *agent provocateur*. He tried again, delivering two more envelopes stuffed with MI5 secrets, which only further convinced the KGB that he was MI5 bait. In exasperation, Bettaney attempted to fly to Vienna, hoping to convince the Austrian-based KGB he was genuine. He was arrested before he left the country.

Bettaney was discovered through information given to MI5 by KGB double agent Oleg Gordievsky. That he had not been identified as a security risk by MI5 testified to a continuing incompetence within the service in terms of ensuring its own security. During Bettaney's growing disaffection, he was convicted of petty crimes, was being treated for alcoholism by an MI5 doctor, and was the subject of two internal enquiries, conducted with each unaware of the other's existence. Yet he continued to be positively vetted and promoted.

Porter notes that Thatcher, 'made a virtue of intolerance'.[13] If there was virtue to be discerned, it was in her unwillingness to let MI5 cover up such gross ineptitude. Her handling of the Bettaney affair differed in two major respects from how her predecessors might have dealt with it. First, she insisted that Bettaney be publicly charged, making Bettaney the first MI5 officer ever to appear in the dock. He attempted to use his trial as a platform for his criticisms about the politicisation of MI5, but was thwarted in so far as the prosecution used all the cloak-and-dagger tactics available to ensure a guilty verdict. The jury was vetted, large portions of the trial were conducted *in camera*, key witnesses were not allowed to be cross-examined and important documents judged inadmissible. With Attorney General Michael Havers leading the prosecution team, Bettaney was jailed for 23 years. Nevertheless, the fact that Bettaney was dealt with publicly constituted a small democratic advance.

A second small advance was Thatcher's decision to convene a Security Commission to investigate MI5 shortcomings. The outcome of this inquiry was mixed as MI5 fought a rearguard action to protect its interests:

> Within the service, the Commission was treated with derision ... When Commission members did make the occasional visit to MI5 headquarters ... officers received advance warning and cleared their desks of sensitive files. Material was deliberately withheld, and some details of Bettaney's uncovering and ... arrest included disinformation.[14]

Overall, the Bettaney case did represent a limited freeing of political discourse about the national security state. Evidence emerged about the state of service morale, unease about the targeting of leftist groups, and the increasing practice of using MI5 to monitor journalists and instigate leaks enquiries. The Security Commission report turned out to be surprisingly critical, in spite of MI5's attempts to gloss its behaviour, although it still pulled its punches. While MI5 management was in a mess, it found MI5's 'professional and operational efficiency' beyond reproach. MI5 head Sir John Jones became the scapegoat and was forced to step down.

For its part, the Commission refused to take Bettaney's criticisms seriously, preferring to focus on his personal shortcomings. Bettaney's criticisms were similarly dismissed by a tabloid media that presented them as 'the ravings of a disturbed individual'.[15] His difficulty in provoking serious public debate about the role of the security and intelligence services mirrors the fate of similar 'challengers' from the margins of the state.

Beginning with the revelations over Blunt and followed more forcibly through the fiasco over Michael Bettaney and then a growing litany of security failures, the Thatcher hard line on security forced MI5 performance into the public eye. In the deepening Cold War context of the early 1980s, the security and intelligence services were engrossed in their main job of catching spies, but their success rate *vis-à-vis* the 'real' enemy – that is, the Eastern Bloc – was poor. While numerous scandals were uncovered and a number of spies wound up in jail, security and intelligence service efforts contributed little to the actual business of catching spies. For all its surveillance, vetting, communications interception and general intriguing, the British counterespionage effort did not produce results. In spite of its wide – and expanding – licence, MI5 in particular seemed utterly incapable of defending the realm, a criticism of its *raison d'être* which called its continued existence into question. On the other hand, given the regularity with which British security was compromised by security service incompetence, it is not difficult to conclude they may have done more harm than good – a suspicion the Americans have long harboured.

Most spies continued to be discovered through information provided by defectors, and that information usually came via other Western channels. In 1986 East German agents Reinhold and Sonia Schulze were arrested in Britain after the West German counter-intelligence head defected to the Eastern Bloc, compromising Western counterespionage operations. The Schultzes were convicted on the possession of spying equipment and false passports and sentenced to ten years for acts preparatory to the commission of espionage offences, a sentence indicative less of the strength of the case against them than of the power of the OSA to achieve harsh results. Despite extensive monitoring efforts by MI5 and GCHQ, the nature and extent of the Schultzes' activities were vague. The trial judge was perhaps making an inadvertent comment on security service performance when he told the Schultzes 'Whether you have communicated secrets and caused actual damage to this country is not known.'[16]

Geoffrey Prime, one of Britain's most notorious postwar spies, was turned in to the police by his wife in 1982. Prime was a Russian linguist in GCHQ who had been recruited by the Soviets while he was still in the RAF; they encouraged him to apply for a job with GCHQ, where he fed signals intelligence (sigint) to the USSR from 1968 until he retired in 1978. In 1982, following police questioning in a child molesting investigation, Prime confessed the sexual offences to his wife and told her about his secret life as a Soviet spy. He pleaded guilty to seven section 1 offences and received a 35-year sentence for espionage and three years for sex offences.

Similarly, the security and intelligence services could not take credit for the netting of Hugh Hambleton, who received a ten-year sentence in 1982. Hambleton passed thousands of crucial Nato documents to the Soviets over 30 years of sporadic spying, including an estimated 80 'cosmic' (the highest security rating) documents.[17] A Canadian economics professor, Hambleton had been arrested in Canada in 1979 for espionage but released for lack of evidence (there was nothing the Canadian government hated more than an espionage case). The British had less compunction and arrested Hambleton when he visited the UK. Hambleton stupidly spoke freely to his Special Branch interrogators, thereby providing them with the bulk of the prosecution's evidence.

The largest security debacle of the 1980s, however, involved the acquittal of nine RAF and army personnel on espionage charges. In 1984, the first case to go to trial involved Paul Davies, an RAF telegraphist for the 12 Signal Unit at the Nato communications centre in Cyprus.[18] Davies was accused of passing classified sigint about RAF jet movements during the Lebanon crisis to a Hungarian woman, Eva Jaafer, married to a Lebanese. Davies had allegedly been compromised through a sex and photos 'honeytrap' operation. The prosecution case teetered when Davies claimed his signed confession had been forced by RAF police, and collapsed when Jaafer appeared as a defence witness. Although she had been under surveillance for the previous 18 months, the prosecution could offer no evidence that she was an enemy agent.

Despite the failure of the Davies case, British intelligence remained convinced that something was going on at the Cyprus post. The following year a case was brought when women's tights and compromising photographs were discovered in the room of a member of the resident Signals unit.[19] Charges were laid against eight members of the unit, alleging they had committed 31 OSA offences between February 1982 and February 1983. On the first day of the trial, one signalman was acquitted when the prosecution offered no evidence; some 120 days later, his codefendants were also acquitted, having spent two years on remand.

The lengthy court trial was held almost completely *in camera*, save for the opening statements and the evidence offered by three defence witnesses. In his opening statement, prosecutor Michael Wright promised a titillating tale of homosexual orgies, blackmail and intrigue. The orgies, which Wright claimed were known as 'splash parties', 'included such practices as dressing up in women's tights, mutual masturbation, oral sex and buggery'. Blackmailed by the KGB, the accused allegedly 'betrayed some of this country's most precious secrets'.[20] Defence witnesses were called to attest to the masculinity and heterosexuality of the defendants, and then the doors closed on the proceedings for several months. On day 107, when it emerged that the defendants had been forced to make confessions, the jury acquitted all seven. *The Times* correspondent wrote: 'From the beginning of the Cyprus spy trial, the Crown offered no evidence in public that there was any proof of a leak of information from 9 Signals Regiment other than what was said in the defendants' statements.'[21] While the prosecution claimed that the defendants had removed secret documents 'by the sackful', no documents were ever found to be missing from the base.

A commission was convened to find out what had gone so badly wrong, and evidence of solitary confinement, threats and psychological duress during the interrogations emerged. The Calcutt Inquiry eventually concluded that the men had been held in oppressive conditions.[22] Thatcher ordered a worldwide investigation into security at all British top secret listening posts scattered around the globe, but the Americans remained unimpressed by this latest example of British ineptitude. American recalcitrance to tender Star Wars research in the UK was blamed on the Cyprus fiasco, the longest and most expensive espionage trial in British history.

If the secret state was suffering from growing public antipathy towards it, then that wound was largely inflicted by the Thatcher government's unwillingness to accept quiet, internally brokered solutions to problems or to leave well enough alone. Characteristic of the government's more brazen approach was the decision to ban trade unionism at GCHQ in 1984. GCHQ industrial action cost an estimated 10,000 lost working days between 1979 and 1981, and the government wanted to bring its employees to heel.[23] To do so, it first had to admit officially that GCHQ existed. The resultant battle over the denial of trade union rights again pushed debate into the public arena, where the government was again embarrassed. The unions involved lodged a complaint at the International Labour Organization (ILO), a UN-related body that has the purpose of prescribing and enforcing minimum labour standards. The ILO found that the government had violated its employees' rights of freedom of association. The government ignored the ruling and the ILO lacked the ability to enforce it. Nevertheless, the mere existance of an independent forum where government actions can be assessed represents a diffusion of political power beyond state borders and holds out the possibility for citizens that their rights could be protected, if not by their own governments, then by international bodies.

International actions such as this pointed to the possibility that those who were traditionally powerless against the national security state now had an avenue of redress. In a changing international context, the political world was now a wider place than the British state. The growing awareness of human rights issues, and in particular the ability of the European Court of Human Rights (ECHR) to intervene on behalf of individuals battling the state, even in matters of national security, curtailed some of the excesses of the security and intelligence services and ultimately provided the external impetus for reform. NCCL members Harman and Hewitt failed in Britain to get a judicial review of their case undertaken, but successfully took a complaint against MI5's surveillance of them to the ECHR. The European Court ruled that, under rights concerning the guarantee to privacy, the files that MI5 held on them should be destroyed – which they were not. However, even if these standards were unenforceable, at least they transcended the traditional elite/mass schisms of British rule with groups now able to arbitrate in areas where state needs and individual rights conflicted. Thus the Thatcher government's trampling of political freedoms led to raised awareness about what citizens have the right to demand of their governments. The rising prominence of organisations such as Liberty and Charter 88 were tangible responses to the assault on civil liberties, as was the sudden influx of politically astute films.

The media versus the government

The interests of the media hitherto had almost invariably coincided with the interests of the government, hence their unwillingness to take on a true adversarial role. However, in the face of Thatcher's authoritarianism, the media were forced to go on the attack, and so discovered their own political efficacy. They became the vehicle by which power struggles at the centre of the state were amplified. Disaffected mandarins like Clive Ponting, Cathy Massiter and Peter Wright all recognised that their greatest weapon against the government was publicity; when they moved to exploit this power, the government responded by trying to muzzle the media, an action that was bound to add fuel to the fire. The government countered increased media criticism by demonstrating the resilience of the laws it had at its disposal, and the courts willingly assisted by interpreting such laws in favour of the government's view of things. The stage was thus set for a battle, with the Thatcher government attempting to enforce limits on media power and the media resisting.

The wide powers of the OSA made it useful for threatening and harassing whistleblowers, but, wary of the press debacles of the 1970s, the state avoided taking newspapers to court for unauthorised disclosure where possible, preferring to rely on libel laws, threats and injunctions. In spite of the extraordinary lengths the Thatcher government went to in order to suppress information, there were just two minor OSA cases brought against the press. In 1981 a police officer was convicted and fined for attempting to sell information about the police hunt for the Yorkshire Ripper to a journalist.[24] And in 1987, journalist John Lee found some police files about a convicted rapist left in a hotel bar. He was acquitted because the prosecution failed to prove he knew the files were covered by the OSA.[25]

The OSA proved more useful in providing the legal justification for harassment than for meting out justice in the courts. In 1987 it was used to coerce the BBC into banning a film about GCHQ, made by Duncan Campbell, which claimed that the MoD had misled parliament by undertaking a £500 million electronic surveillance project without informing the House as was required.[26] The BBC denied that there had been any government pressure to withdraw the film, but in turn, citing copyright violations, refused to allow Campbell to show the film to MPs in a private screening or to hold illegal 'guerrilla screenings' around the country.

Campbell refused to buckle to BBC pressure, or to the pressure being applied by the government to prevent his allegations from being made public. The Attorney General failed to win a court injunction to prevent MPs from watching the film, but persuaded the Speaker of the House to ban it and won an injunction to prevent Campbell from discussing the contents of his film. Newspapers were formally warned to steer clear.

Campbell defied the injunctions and published his information in the *New Statesman*. The state response was vindictive: the Special Branch arrived with warrants issued under the OSA to carry out random searches at Campbell's home, a film researcher's home and the *New Statesman* offices. A week later, this time with an illegal warrant, ten police officers raided the BBC's Scottish office where they conducted a 28-hour search and removed several vanloads of film, videos and documentation. The harassment of the BBC was seen as particularly unfair given that the BBC had been so cooperative in trying to silence Campbell.

Although the government succeeded in quashing the actual film, Campbell managed to get the story out, but only because he was willing to defy official pressure and risk prosecution. Within the centre of the state, however, he found little sympathy or assistance at the various nodes that had the power to help him. The legal-rational state did not have the capacity to assist the whistleblower, enslaved as it was to the policy dictates of the centre. The Speaker's decision to prevent the film being shown to MPs, the judiciary's willingness to grant injunctions and warrants, the Special Branch's willingness to harass those involved, and the BBC's willingness to ban the film were indicators of the powers ranged against Campbell, the lone whistleblower on the margins. At the centre of the state, the orthodoxy held surprisingly well, in spite of Thatcher's controversial programmes. If the government said the film threatened national security, then no legal-rational institution was going to question that claim. Two years later, the BBC finally aired the film, without mishap, either to itself or, apparently, to British security.

The most notorious battle between the press and official secrecy did not involve the OSA at all, but it did once again involve a figure on the margins of the secret state. The government spent three years and over £2 million in litigation in its failed attempt to prevent the British public from reading Peter Wright's autobiography, *Spycatcher*. This massive effort is generally viewed as misguided fiasco, but the stakes the government was playing for were of the highest order: as the *Guardian* put it, the government sought nothing less than to prevent disclosure of 'any information, ever, obtained from former members of the security and intelligence services'.[27] And while the government ultimately lost this battle – *Spycatcher* was published – it does not follow that it lost the war.

The government used a number of legal tactics to quash the book, beginning by seeking an injunction against publication in Australia (where Wright lived) in September 1985. In June 1986 the *Guardian* and the *Observer* published articles concerning the upcoming trial and were hastily banned from making further reports under laws regarding confidentiality. Nine months later, the *Independent* led other papers in publishing further disclosures and all were charged with contempt of court, even though they were not covered by the June injunction. A glut of court proceedings ensued. 'It was an alarming and unprecedented sight,' says David Hooper, 'to see six newspapers prosecuted for contempt of court with two others being proceeded against for breach of confidence'.[28]

In 1988 the Law Lords found that Wright, along with all former members of the security services, owed a lifelong duty of confidence to the Crown – a finding later to be enshrined in the Security Services Act. But, as it had been published outside the UK, *Spycatcher* had sold 2 million copies and so the court decided that domestic publication could not now damage national security further. This ruling was based on purely pragmatic considerations – the fact that the book was widely available – and had nothing to do with the issues of official secrecy or security service accountability. Nevertheless, the court's finding was celebrated with a headline across the front page of the *Guardian* that claimed 'Press wins Spycatcher battle':

> Make no mistake, this is a significant victory for press freedom and for newspapers which have plugged away at the issues for over two years now. The Government has tried every legal device to gag publication of the memoirs and suppress discussion of the grave allegations they make. Now we can get on and do our job.[29]

Others were more cautious. Peter Kellner of the *Observer* described the outcome of the legal wrangles as a pyrrhic victory because two important legal precedents had been established.[30] First, the Court of Appeal ruled that an injunction against one media outlet applied to all – hence the birth of the blanket injunction, which the Law Lords further widened to apply to bans on the reporting of Australian legal proceedings in the British press. Second, the law of confidentiality was found to extend to the media.

In 1990 the European Court of Human Rights overturned this last ruling, finding that the injunctions brought against the *Observer* and the *Guardian* violated freedom of expression as defined under article 10 of the Convention for the Protection of Human Rights and Fundamental Freedoms. Like the Law Lords, the ECHR found that the wide availability of the material made the injunctions redundant; more importantly, the ECHR did find that 'the English courts did not give sufficient weight to the public's right to know about the workings of government and the duty of the press to denounce misconduct by a government authority'.[31] The most significant implication of the ruling was that the principle of the public interest was found to be more important than the absolute duty of confidentiality, particularly when the activities of government officials were involved. This, Richard Norton-Taylor said, challenged two points of English law: 'prior restraint', used to restrict the media before publication, and the 1989 OSA controls on what the media are allowed to publish about the security services.[32]

Somewhere in the fog surrounding the media disputes over government gag orders, the impact of Wright's insider's view of MI5 was lost. Stephen Dorril described *Spycatcher* as 'probably one of the most important books to be published about Britain since the Second World War', but argues that the British media 'did little more than regurgitate sections'.[33] Wright's most spectacular revelations – MI5 plots to assassinate the Egyptian president, Gamal Nasser; fear within the service that former MI5 head Roger Hollis was a Soviet mole; and, most disturbingly, the existence of a renegade group within MI5 that had tried to destabilise the Wilson government – received a great deal of attention, but these disclosures went further than most people were prepared to believe. Wright's suggestion that groups operated within the British state with sufficient power and will to destabilise Wilson, for example, was widely dismissed as ridiculous. Scepticism surrounding the book was partly orchestrated by MI5 itself, which issued a briefing paper carefully refuting Wright's allegations line by line. Such tactics fed into negative publicity about the quality of the book and the factual errors it contained, making it easier to discredit. That Peter Wright was a man in a funny hat who had been embroiled in a pension dispute with Her Majesty's Government contributed to his image as a crank. Like Massiter, whose mental health was questioned by her superiors, and Bettaney, whose personal defects were officially emphasised, Wright's whistleblowing could be discounted as the act of a troubled or embittered person. The state attempted to force Clive Ponting into this category as well: his interest in Buddhism and that he was going 'through a bad patch' were cited as reasons for his leak.[34] 'Normal' people do not rock the boat.

The incredulity surrounding Wright's allegations suited the state. Public awareness of MI5's bungling and burgling exploits should have provided a strong argument for greater accountability. Instead, discredited, Wright's book simply became another piece in the mosaic of half-truths, untruths and uncorroborated accounts that comprise public knowledge of the secret state.

The civil service: the Ponting case

Although prosecutions of civil servants under the OSA are common, they usually occur at the margins of the system, among the lower echelons who are less tied into the bureaucratic structure and do not have a great career stake in it. Such offenders are seldom considered important enough to be taken seriously by the media. They are useful as scapegoats and examples, but in the great scheme of things they are dispensable and easily forgotten. In 1982 Rhona Ritchie, a second secretary at the British embassy in Tel Aviv, was given a nine-month suspended sentence for giving official information to a member of the Egyptian embassy with whom she was romantically involved. The Attorney-General described her crime as 'more foolish than wicked'.[35] Usually such an offence would have been disciplined internally, as even the Foreign Office claimed no harm had been done, but one document Ritchie passed involved correspondence between Lord Carrington and the American General Alexander Haig. Ritchie was charged because the UK needed to appear tough on leaks to assuage perennial American doubts about British security. In another case, in 1985 two company directors and two MoD officials were charged with unauthorised disclosure, as well as with bribery and other offences, for investigating the possibility of supplying Argentina with Rolls-Royce aircraft engines. The two civil servants were initially acquitted at a magistrate's hearing, but the charges were reinstated and the matter taken to the Crown Court. One defendant eventually received a two-year sentence, but this was quashed on appeal when the appellant successfully argued that the MoD had tacitly authorised the communication of the information; the other civil servant received twelve months.[36]

Therefore, the most unusual aspect of the 1984 decision to prosecute Clive Ponting for leaking official information was his position as a senior mandarin working at the policy-making centre of the British state. Examples of high-level whistleblowing are rare and transgressions are almost always dealt with behind closed doors; the Thatcher government made a serious tactical error when it chose to fight Ponting through the public arena of the courts, rather than letting him leave the service quietly. Whereas Peter Wright's insider's view of the strange world of MI5 could be discredited, it was more difficult to dismiss public criticisms made by a senior Whitehall mandarin. By deciding to fight, the government pitted itself against two now powerful political adversaries, the media and the civil service. Ponting realised the importance of public opinion to his case and made a point of occupying the moral high ground early.

As the manoeuvring of the internal dispute spilled into the media, the public was given unprecedented views into how power works at the political centre. Ponting's specific offence was to make unauthorised disclosures about the circumstances surrounding the sinking of the Argentinian warship, the *General Belgrano*, but his action was born both of long-term disaffection within Whitehall, where he felt he did not 'fit in', and of his growing dissatisfaction with the Thatcher government's policies towards the civil service.

Ponting's disaffection was indicative of how little it takes to be 'different' in Whitehall and how difficult it is to express these differences by, for example, articulating positions that run against the prevailing grain. Ponting saw himself as an outsider, and, indeed, a glance at Whitehall recruitment statistics would suggest he was correct to think himself so. A Reading graduate, he initially decided against a civil service career on the grounds that 'it was probably full of people from Oxbridge'.[37] In this sense, like Wright, who felt marginalised because he did not read classics at Oxbridge, and Bettaney the working-class Catholic, Ponting to some extent represented the margins of the centre. He saw himself as an ideal bureaucratic type, rational and pragmatic, in contrast to the clubby Victorian mentality that pervaded Whitehall, where mandarins worked to protect and further their own interests, not to carry out government policies.

Initially, Ponting's own misgivings about the civil service dovetailed with Thatcher's desire to reform it, and he received an OBE from Thatcher for his chronicling of bureaucratic waste and inefficiency as part of an early Thatcher reform campaign. His actions were significantly less popular among his MoD colleagues, who sent him on paid leave as a 'punishment' for his criticisms. Thatcher intervened to have him reinstated. But his enthusiasm for Thatcher's reforms waned as Ponting began to feel the objective of the changes was to swap one set of unsavoury values for another. Instead of a more rational, more efficient bureaucracy, Ponting saw one that was becoming increasingly politicised: 'a greater degree of political commitment to the policies of the Government was expected', he wrote. 'Loyalty and not the ability to produce well-reasoned argument was to be the chief characteristic of the new breed of top civil servants.'[38]

Ponting's moment of crisis came when he was asked to participate in the government's cover-up of the 1982 sinking of the *General Belgrano*, which had been blown up during the Falklands War with a loss of 368 men. The *Belgrano* had been sunk in mysterious circumstances: it was outside the declared British maritime exclusion zone surrounding the Falklands and eleven hours into a journey away from the proscribed area. There were suspicions that the sinking was illegal under international law. Questions were raised in the House about the circumstances of the sinking and, when asked to draft disingenuous answers, Ponting balked: 'I found myself wondering whether the Civil Service was really going to be party to the deliberate deception of Parliament simply to try to preserve the illusion that Ministers had told the truth and thus protect their political reputation.'[39] He sent an anonymous letter and some unclassified MoD documents to Tam Dalyell MP, who was pursuing the affair. Unlike Tisdall, Ponting moved precisely within what he thought were the acceptable parameters of legality. By sending the documents to an MP, it was uncertain whether an offence had been committed (precedent would suggest not), and in any case he was careful to reveal information that would not damage national security. As he later explained, 'I could not, to be frank, bring myself to disclose Government information.'[40] Within weeks he took the highly unusual step of requesting a transfer out of the MoD.

When Ponting was identified as the source of the leak, senior mandarins worked hard to persuade Michael Heseltine not to press charges. Whitehall tried to protect Ponting, not because it agreed with his action but because it did not want its mistakes in handling the affair to come out. Ponting's whistleblowing exposed civil service incompetence in the area of security: he had been left in a position with access to highly secret information even after he had requested a transfer out of the MoD, his disaffection known. He was a textbook security risk. It also exposed the willingness of other mandarins to follow the government line and assist in the cover-up. A senior MoD police officer told Ponting

> The department does not come out of this very well and they want it all cleared up quickly. Nobody has told the Prime Minister yet. It has been agreed that if you are prepared to resign then that will be the end of the matter.[41]

Certainly Ponting had no wish to become a folk hero; he was worried about his future prospects and 'felt that if I was to resign it was important to find out what sort of reference I would get'.[42] A gentlemen's agreement was struck between Ponting and his superiors by which Ponting would resign and receive a good reference.

Under previous governments, this might well have been the end of the affair, but, while the department was hoping to sweep the matter under the carpet, a government rapidly earning a reputation for brooking no leaks proved recalcitrant. Aware of the double standard the mandarins were trying to enforce by charging Tisdall while allowing Ponting to resign, Heseltine refused to make allowances. If an offence had been committed, Ponting would be charged. What Whitehall knew, and what the Thatcher government failed to appreciate, was how much damage a vindictive civil servant can do once he has lost his stake in the system.

Gaining a conviction was always going to be an uphill battle. In the past, leaking directly to parliament had not led to OSA charges, and, given the careful nature of Ponting's information, the usual arguments about national security lacked potency. Working from within the system, Ponting had exposed the questionable basis of the state's 'national security' blanket. The prosecution opted to argue that Ponting committed a straightforward breach of confidentiality, an offence Ponting admitted. The prosecution anticipated an easy victory in a magistrate's court, much like Tisdall's. Instead, Ponting pleaded not guilty and mounted a full-scale media campaign to establish that, while he had indeed committed an offence, he had acted in the public interest.

The so-called public interest defence is embedded in section 2 of the Official Secrets Act, which stipulates that it is an offence if a Crown servant:

> communicates the code word, pass word, sketch, plan, model, article, note, document, or information to any person, other than a person to whom he is authorised to communicate it, *or a person to whom it is in the interest of the State his duty to communicate it.* [My emphasis]

Ponting argued that his action was justified because he was exposing government's abuse of power and that therefore it was in the wider interests of the state that the information be revealed. Whatever its moral desirability, certainly this interpretation of the 'public interest defence' had never been recognised, with two previous failed attempts to establish such a definition. In 1940 a naval officer used the same argument when he was charged with sending nonsecret information to his brother, a reporter for a communist newspaper. The defence counsel argued that the accused had acted 'in their view very much in the interests of the state and to expose a breach by the authorities of an undertaking of a Minister of the Crown'.[43] The magistrate remarked that the same could be said of any traitor and sentenced the officer to twelve months and his journalist brother to six months.

The most important attempt to clarify the ambiguity surrounding the 'interest of the State' clause was the Committee of 100's appeal case in 1962. Five antinuclear campaigners had been convicted under the espionage section of the OSA for unauthorised entry to RAF Wetherfield, where their presence disabled the airfield. The appellants argued that it was not their civil disobedience at the airfield that threatened the state; rather, the mere presence of nuclear weapons on British soil was the greatest threat to national security and their actions were performed 'in the interests of the State' to alleviate this threat.[44]

Their convictions were upheld on the grounds that in national defence, 'the Crown alone was entitled to decide the disposition and order of the armed forces, and the propriety of the decision on such matters could not be questioned in a court of law'.[45] In essence, it was up to the government of the day to decide what policy was in the interests of the state. Ergo, since the government had decided that nuclear weapons at Wetherfield were in the nation's interests, their policy could not be challenged. Ponting's defence stressed that the difference between his disclosure and the Committee of 100's civil disobedience was that Ponting had emphatically not harmed national security. The defence argued that there was a lawful place for acting in the interests of the state as opposed to the interests of the government, if, as in this case, the government was lying to parliament, and national security was not jeopardised by revelation.

Thomas has argued that it may be incorrect to interpret the phrase 'interest of the State' in section 2 as 'the public interest'. 'The public interest' suggests a duty that transcends one's official responsibilities, whereas the phrase 'in the interest of the State' exists 'to permit the accused to show an affirmative official duty to communicate the information to the person who received it'.[46] Justice McCowan, the judge hearing Ponting's case, strengthened this interpretation by ruling that the only legal way to communicate information was if it was authorised or part of an official duty. He held that the interests of the state were indeed the policies of the government of the day and that Ponting's duty was an official duty to serve his ministers, not to serve some civic or moral duty that he felt personally to be in the public interest. This was by no means a radical position, but the ruling underscored the fact that in Britain it remains all but impossible to challenge the state's views on national security because of the extent of the government's prerogative in decision-making. Official silence on the *Belgrano* issue had been justified through reference to national security; without knowing the basis upon which the policy was being decided, individual challenges could not be sustained, as Ponting discovered.

In straightforward legal terms, then, Ponting was guilty. His acquittal was not won on the strength of his legal position but by persuading the jury of the morality of his action – an interesting conclusion to a case he has tried to base on his unswerving adherence to 'rational' administration. If the British state did function rationally, Ponting would have been found guilty, legal precedents regarding disclosure would have been strengthened and the government would have yet another deterrent example to chill civil servants into silence. The unprecedented acquittal instead rendered the OSA useless as a tool for silencing mandarins, leading to its 1989 replacement with a new Act that conveniently removed the public interest defence.

Ponting's acquittal is usually seen as one in which moral right and individual integrity win out in spite of 'bad' laws like the OSA. When Ponting fell foul of the legal and political system, he was acquitted by a jury, a reassuring check to a politically-motivated application of the OSA by a vindicative government. Such a view posits a static, reliable and rational state from which a 'just' outcome emerges. Here, the Thatcher government's miscalculation was the extent of the jury's sympathy for Ponting and its unwillingness to be persuaded by the traditionally foolproof national security argument advanced by the state. Thus Ponting's acquittal has been used to suggest that the structures of the state function effectively, legitimating rather than challenging the liberal view of the state. Nevertheless, aside from the acquittal itself, positive results are hard to discern. While government ministers who had misled parliament were exposed, this had little noticeable effect on their subsequent careers. The OSA was by now thoroughly discredited, but its reputation was already in tatters and the government was using different legislation and enacting new laws to achieve the same effects. Civil servants' codes were tightened and new practices for accommodating conscience-stricken mandarins were set up, to little effect. The irony is that, like the press 'victory' in the *Spycatcher* affair, Ponting's actions led to a tightening rather than a loosening of the state's control over information.

The secret state at the end of the 1980s was radically different from the one that existed when Thatcher was elected in 1979. While the new legislation was rewritten in favour of the state, and in particular the secret state, the fact that it was written at all meant that the citizenry no longer had to tilt at wraiths. There are now genuine pieces of legislation to wring one's hands over: the Security Services Act 1989; the Official Secrets Act 1989; the Public Order Act 1986; the Intelligence Services Act 1993. There is now accountability, albeit limited and inadequate, where there was none before. There are fewer rights protected and loopholes to escape from in the legislation, yet there remains the possibility of challenging and changing these weaknesses. If the Foucauldian dictate holds true that resistance rises at the points of greatest oppression, the weaknesses of these laws in civil rights terms may yet be addressed.

The laws themselves are indicative of the huge gap between elites and masses in policy-making, and how closed policy-making leads to laws that simply perpetuate the powers of those who make the laws at the expense of those whose interests the laws are meant to protect. It was the security services themselves that sought legislation, deciding it was better to enact limited reforms sooner than have more sweeping reforms thrust upon them later. The Security Services Bill, drafted by MI5 lawyers, gave the service 'the minimum legal framework that would allow the service to operate much as it had done in the past'.[47] Likewise, the new OSA made it more difficult for whistleblowers to escape conviction.

The real legacy of the Thatcher period was the insight provided into the secret state and the identification of sites where resistance was possible. As the Thatcher government sought to tighten internal security and limit political dissent by widening its definition of subversion, it encountered impediments both at the centre and at the margins of the demos. With social polarisation came knowledge of the arcane working of the secret state. Clive Ponting's whistleblowing provided a rare glimpse into the secretive workings of Whitehall; Peter Wright revealed the power and ignominy of the security services. Post-Thatcherite Britain may be less free than it was, but the configuration of its freedoms and lacks are more clearly delineated as a result. That in the mid-1990s constitutional reform appeared on the political agenda is a product of the change in the national consciousness. Whether the state is resilient enough to resist genuine change, its anti-democratic tendencies able to slip the knot of political reform, remains to be seen.

CHAPTER 7

THE BRITISH STATE AND THE FUTURE OF SECRECY

> It has all the hallmarks of an authoritarian state in which power
> resides in the hands of officials with no democratic or legal mecha-
> nisms to call them to account.
>
> Tony Bunyan[1]

Readers might well by this point assume that the above epigraph
refers to the United Kingdom. However, while Britons continue
to attempt to improve the British state by putting constitutional
change on the agenda, pushing for more open and accountable
government or turning to nongovernmental and/or international
bodies to protect the rights of citizens, the quotation actually
refers to a secret state being erected at a higher level: the new
leviathan presently stalking British democracy might well be the
European Union. On the other hand, the EU might instead be
the great liberating force, freeing British democracy from the
shackles of the excessive secrecy and narrowness of its national
ruling culture. The point is that political power is already shifting away from the nation-state and finding new networks
through which to flow. Concepts of citizenship are being re-
shaped by the global marketplace of goods and ideas, and the
idea of a citizenship based on loyalty to a nation-state is fast
becoming redundant – even as troubled governments and groups
try to reinvigorate creeds of nationalism in order to engender
new kinds of legitimacy and certainty in an increasingly anarchic
world. Whether such shifts will lead to political empowerment or
further de-democratisation is still unclear. What is clear is that,
by concentrating on reforming the structures of the legal-rational
state, we risk losing sight of the way in which power is transformed with transformations of the system. New (or, in some
cases, the same) ruling elites will redeploy political power in new
ways in order to shape, encourage or, as is usually the case, limit
the political discourses of the demos.

It is no longer enough simply to rethink the British state as a
solution to the problems of de-democratisation. Debates about
national security and particularly the nature of threat will continue

to influence the relationship between citizens and governments, but of course 'national' security, already indivisible from international security during the Cold War, is now bound up with the security concerns of a confused post-Cold War world. The UK, its traditional allies, and European states both East and West, have been retrenching their security policies in light of the new realities of international relations. We have seen states retrench before: we have seen how the British centre was able to mould policies that targeted and discredited the left after the First and Second World Wars, and how, by defining threat in particular ways and then using the legal-rational state and the rhetoric of national security to police those definitions, it was able to manipulate the British polity in ways that furthered its own interests at the expense of the wider population. The question facing policy-makers – and the citizens they administer – is what form the world is taking as it lurches towards the twenty-first century.

For the relationship between security and democracy in the so-called New World Order, the major issues involve how threat is defined, how states react to these new threats, and whether citizens can mount effective resistance when their rights are violated or threatened. In this period of transition, where threats are multiple, and actions and reactions fluid, the danger is that the New World Order will deliver not new, improved forms of liberty and freedom, but merely more refined methods of social control. There are contradictory trends. On the one hand, citizens have greater and wider access to a plurality of information sources through the advances of the much heralded Information Age. They are better informed, better organised and have the potential to forge new networks of discourse across national, cultural and economic borders. On the other hand, there are signs that information manipulation is becoming increasingly sophisticated and that the postmodern dilemma is one in which uncertainty and consequent inertia become the characteristic contemporary states engendered precisely by the proliferation of competing information sources.

New threats into old bottles

With the sudden demise of the Soviet Union, the unexpected collapse of the East/West binary that had defined political loyalties so categorically since the end of the Second World War (if not for most of the twentieth century) left international security in a vacuum. That security and intelligence services, along with political scientists and virtually everyone else, failed to predict the end of the Soviet Union rendered the whole project of threat assessment somewhat suspect (a failure compounded by Western governments' failure to foresee the Iraqi invasion of Kuwait in 1990). Nevertheless, the confidence of those whose job it is to persuade policy-makers of how best to secure the state against threat was not shaken for long. Even as the Berlin Wall was being dismantled, the search was on for a new threat, not just as a matter of contingency planning for national and international security, but as a matter of survival for those whose interests are bound up with government defence budgets. The problem was – and remains – that post-Soviet threats are not clear cut. Myriad new contenders have arrived on the playing field now emptied of communist revolutionaries: terrorists; Islamic fundamentalists; drugs traffickers; even immigrants, as political analysts posited that hordes of dispossessed Eastern Bloc citizens, now granted freedom, would flow to the West to claim the glittering prizes that capitalism offered.

For the national security apparatuses, the search for a new threat has mirrored the desperate search for a *raison d'être* after the First World War when, with the German defeat, budgets were slashed and the secret state rolled back to peacetime proportions. In Britain, MI5 quickly moved to establish a stronger beachhead in the task of combatting terrorism by moving its resources away from countersubversion and politicking behind the scenes to get the government executive and Whitehall to agree to an enhanced post-Cold War role. 'The stakes were high', notes Stephen Dorril; 'failure in this enterprise would expose the service to the threat of disbandment. It had no where else to go.'[2] But MI5 was treading on territory already occupied by the Special Branch, the Anti-Terrorist Squad and MI6. The operational failures of these other groups provided MI5's ammunition: MI6 was in the doghouse for its failure to detect arms shipments from Libya to the IRA; Special Branch foul-ups led to the escape of two IRA suspects from Brixton Prison in 1991 (although the Special Branch blamed MI5 involvement). There were even allegations that MI5 mounted a black propaganda campaign to make the police look bad at this crucial juncture. MI5 was also able to capitalise on its ability to access Whitehall and government ministers whereas the police lack such political clout.

In the end, MI5 lobbying has been successful: in 1991 policy-makers decided to award MI5 an enhanced counterterrorism role. The police were, of course, bitter at being stripped of some of their powers in this arena, but the specific objections they raised concerning MI5's record on protecting civil liberties while carrying out its tasks are genuine. In 1992 police sources complained to the *Guardian* that: 'The only extra tactics which MI5 could employ would be illegal. We are a great deal more open and accountable than MI5.'[3]

'If they get terrorism, drugs will be next', a senior police officer warned.[4] As a potential security threat, drugs were proving to be a popular cause in the United States, which had until recently little direct experience of terrorist activity. By 1988 sectors of the American defence establishment were already initiating a 'War on Drugs' which paved the way for the US invasion of Panama in 1989. MI5 continues its politicking in the hope of gaining responsibility for operations against drugs, money-laundering and organised crime, thereby creating for itself a powerful role in Europe, a highly desirable goal for a secret service that most Britons would like to see disbanded. It is an ironic comment on British policy-making that it is this most suspect and unaccountable organ of the British secret state that is being successful in forging a new role for itself.

The police, on the other hand, having been squeezed out of terrorism have most recently been inventing a new enemy: the environmentalist. In late 1994, the Special Branch announced it was switching its priorities to the green movement and in March 1996 the Anti-Terrorist Squad was turned to the task of gathering intelligence on environmental activists.[5] This was in spite of the fact – admitted by the Association of Chief Police Officers -that no green terrorist offences had taken place and there was no evidence that any were likely to occur.

The changing British state

Such machinations over the British state's responses to the post-Cold War world are indicative of how, behind the window-dressing of the legal-rational state, powerful interest groups are reforming and regrouping in order to maintain their influence in the wake of the Soviet collapse. Even with the old enemy 'defeated', the British state continues to enact laws to protect rather than curb the existing powers of the secret state. Ewing and Gearty reported with alarm the complacence of Sir John Donaldson, Master of the Rolls and senior member of the Court of Appeal who defended the security service's tendencies to act outside of the law. Donaldson suggested 'that it was "absurd" to claim that every breach of the law by the security service amounted to a "wrongdoing"'. Ewing and Gearty found that Donaldson's comments defied one of the 'most fundamental of all the liberal values':

> One of the hallmarks of a democratic and civilised society is that government is conducted in accordance with the rule of law. One of the hallmarks of a totalitarian society is that state officials have unrestrained power. Dicey, no radical by a long chalk, pointed out ... that the rule of law 'excludes the idea of any exemption of officials or others from the duty of obedience to the law which governs other citizens or from the jurisdiction of the ordinary tribunals'.[6]

That MI5, probably the organ most responsible for trampling on civil liberties during the Cold War years, has succeeded in cutting out a new and potentially more powerful role for itself, suggests that the fight to redemocratise the British state is just beginning and that the legal-rational state continues to be a legitimising convenience for policy-makers rather than a democratic safeguard for British citizens.

In the fall-out after the Ponting trial, the Thatcher government finally enacted a new Official Secrets Act which became law in 1989. While the new law was less broadly drawn than the old, and supposedly confined now to information relating to defence, intelligence, policing, international agreements and security rather than the blanket provisions of the 1911 act, critics charged that it could well prove in practice to be more draconian. Most notably, the problematical 'public interest' defence that had swayed Ponting's jury was removed. Whether the new OSA is better or worse than its predecessor remains largely a moot point, as the state has continued to use less controversial legislation to achieve the same ends. While the Conservative government of the past 17 years has seldom appeared to be afraid of controversy, in this respect at least it has not gone looking for trouble. Other laws, like libel and contempt, and other tactics, work just as well and do not have the notorious reputation of the OSA.

The Thatcher government did bring real changes. In some ways the secret state is now less secret; with a new OSA, a Security Services Act, official willingness to admit to the existence of the security and intelligence services and to debate their functions, and governments once again willing to pay lip service to the cause of freedom of information, it has to be admitted that the legal-rational trappings of the British state have been improved. Bernard Porter noted that the Thatcher years saw more hours of parliamentary debate devoted to security service issues than the previous 160 years.[7] Public debate, however slim, at least represents a significant improvement.

The other side of the coin is that change in general for the British state has been for the worse in so far as de-democratisation has continued apace, the continuing legacy of Thatcher's attempts to rewrite the state. In what has been described as 'the exit from politics', citizens have been remoulded as consumers, and politicians as managers. Politics is less the art of negotiation, vision and compromise than a full-scale submission to 'market forces'. Local democracy has been destroyed as local councils have been stripped of their roles, and powers have been increasingly concentrated at the centre. Public institutions have been privatised, submitted to 'market forces', and government functions hived off into unaccountable quangos. This is still further testimony to the inadequacy of focusing on the legal-rational state as the vehicle for delivering improved democracy. On paper, the path to improving the British legal-rational state seems clear; in reality, policy-makers are shape-shifters, able to remodel the state in ways that appear 'democratic' – as in eliding arguments about consumer choice and market forces with political freedom – while in fact creating a state that is less, not more, accountable.

Britain and the European state

In terms of political change, Britain's involvement in the European Union will be the most significant influence upon the nature of the relationship between citizen and state. Institutions like the EU and the UN, in transcending the boundaries of state sovereignty, are possible sites of resistance for a citizenry that cannot always find justice within its own borders. Britain's membership in the European Union is part of a wider trend towards greater globalisation and interdependence, where even debates about official secrecy and national security can transcend national boundaries. As with GCHQ unions taking complaints to the International Labour Organization, NCCL and CND members complaining successfully to the European Court of Human Rights, government attitudes towards national security and the role their citizens play within the security nexus may no longer be left unchallenged by citizens.

But while in many respects the EU promises to empower individuals, in other respects the prospects for the enhanced democratisation that many expect the EU to deliver need to be seen more critically. While the UK remains something of a New Right outpost on the margins of a federated Europe, there is a temptation to look longingly at the EU as the arena in which a more democratic political programmes might be found. The European Union is viewed by many who see Britain's national democratic prospects irrevocably damaged as the arena in which empowerment may occur. Such views underestimate the ability of states, even enlightened and self-conscious creations like the EU, to write their own rules when it comes to handing over democratic power.

In the EU, this is already becoming evident in the setting up of European security policies. Security agreements provide so many provisos and get-out clauses that it is over-optimistic to accept the EU as the answer to British prayers for a more open and democratic society. The European Court of Human Rights promises new hope for preserving and upholding civil liberties in Britain, but, at the same time, the erection of Fortress Europe, with police, immigration, customs officers, civil servants, military and security services increasingly cooperating with little public scrutiny or transparency, could well lead to a more repressive and unaccountable system of control of the European polity. MI5's attempts to re-invent itself and to manoeuvre into a position that would find it placed as Britain's representative at the centre of a new European police state is an uncomfortable reminder that whatever hopes for the EU as a guarantor of democratic rights must be balanced against its potential as a powerful and unaccountable withholder of those rights.

So far, the prognosis has not been very positive. When it came to making official secrecy and vetting policies to protect the emerging European state, European Commission policy-makers looked to the UK as an example.[8] In 1992, regulations were proposed that would provide the same sort of blanket protection of official information that the UK had become infamous for under its *old* Official Secrets Act. While the proposals for secrecy regulations were withdrawn under the reworking of Maastricht's subsidiarity clause in 1992, the provisions that the Commission sought are indicative of the fact that the European state might be evolving towards something as authoritarian, secretive and unaccountable as the British state ever was. The regulations proposed were applicable to any and all areas of EC policy and would have enabled classified information to be categorised as 'all forms of information whose unauthorised disclosure could be detrimental to the essential interests of the European Communities and of Member States'.[9] 'Detrimental' and 'essential interests' were not defined, promising European policy-makers a wide mandate for deciding what to keep secret.

This blanket regulation was withdrawn, but, instead, *ad hoc* arrangements under which the European state has operated since the mid-1970s continue to shroud European-wide policing and security functions in secrecy. Immigration, policing, security and information-sharing are carried out routinely while 'the mechanism for decision-making between the EU states leaves power in the hands of officials (from Interior ministries, police, immigration, customs, and security services)'.[10]

The coordination of policing and security functions in a federated Europe date back to the mid-1970s, when a number of *ad hoc* groups were established to investigate various policy areas including the combatting of terrorism and general police cooperation. Referred to collectively as the Trevi group, since 1976 working groups have been set up to coordinate actions on terrorism, drug trafficking, football hooliganism, organised crime and public order. The mandates of these working groups sound anodyne enough: the major thrust of Trevi was to share information and create avenues for liaison and coordination across a European state with increasingly permeable internal borders. The erection of a policing structure has been justified on the grounds of pooling expertise and making the management and administration of policing more efficient.

Trevi is not within the European Union's mandate, as EU involvement does not extend to policing. Instead, the Trevi group is responsible to the Council of Ministers, that is, it is directly responsible to individual governments. The ministers of the interior who usually represent governments at Trevi meetings supposedly guarantee democratic safeguards. As a British EC minister said, Trevi

> does not need safeguards ... Trevi is merely a gathering together of the Ministers of the Interior of the EC countries, to give, hopefully, political impetus to various plans for closer policing co-operation ... there is no need for the body as a whole to be thought of as responsible to any other organisations.[11]

In the late 1980s EC member states set about creating Europol, an EC-level policing body; its stated mandate is to be a 'central organisation to facilitate the exchange and coordination of criminal information, and the development of intelligence between Member States in respect of crime extending across the borders'.[12] The Maastricht agreement moved these *ad hoc* arrangements onto formal footing, the beginning, Tony Bunyan notes, of EC efforts to combine economic projects that the Common Market represented with the political aspects of statehood. But this newly evolving European state, he argues, lacks the basic tenets of liberal democracy: 'This state has been conceived by governments, honed by state officials, and passed back to governments to agree – only then have national parliaments been asked to ratify the whole package.' The wholesale effect is 'in almost every instance to diminish peoples' rights. No democratic accountability or due process of law to protect the citizen is built in.'[13]

Sharing intelligence and information is at the heart of these organisations, giving rise to the same problems of state surveillance of individuals and the violation of individual rights this entails, but on a much larger scale. There are countless examples of the damage that incorrect intelligence held by the state can inflict on individuals. One particularly compelling European example occurred in the late 1970s, when British industrial filmmaker Jan Martin, employed by a private company contracted to make a promotional film for Taylor-Woodrow, was denied access to Taylor-Woodrow's premises.[14] Routine security vetting had revealed that Martin was a 'security threat' with links to the Baader-Meinhof gang. Because her father was a former Detective Superintendent at Scotland Yard, Martin was able to discover why she had been blacklisted. While on holiday in Holland, a café owner misidentified her husband as a terrorist suspect and phoned the local police. While the police established that they were in fact just tourists, the initial report somehow found its way onto MI5 and Special Branch files. According to their records, Jan Martin consorted with terrorists.

Bunyan notes that the Council of Europe made specific recommendations about how data held on private individuals should be used and stored. The UK objected to recommendations that individuals be informed when information recorded without their knowledge is being held on file, and also rejected a suggestion concerning the prohibition of

> the collection of data on individuals solely on the basis that they have a particular racial origin, particular religious convictions, sexual behaviour or political opinions or belong to particular movements or organisations which are not proscribed by law.[15]

Even this admirable recommendation by the Council of Europe contained a get-out clause: it goes on to read, 'The collection of data concerning these factors may only be carried out if absolutely necessary for the purposes of a particular enquiry.'

The future of secrecy

The manner in which states control information and use their power to shape political discourse has undergone changes in the face of an increasingly anarchic and anonymous world of communication and transmission. But as long as the state – whether it is the British state or a future European superstate or something in between – maintains its preeminence in national security matters, it is able to ward off opposition by withholding ammunition from potential critics. And as long as the political centre views the population in terms of friend or foe, depending on the political discourses individuals engage in, it will continue to use its power to maintain its own position at the expense of its citizens.

To reverse the de-democratisation process requires more than tinkering with the legal-rational state. Britons worried about the changing nature of the state under Thatcher have laid the blame at the peculiar lack of constitutional guarantees which has meant that executive power has frequently gone unchallenged when curbs have been needed. However, as Tony Wright points out, the problem is far more deeply rooted than that. He notes that the Thatcher government did not subvert the rules of governance to achieve antidemocratic ends; it simply stretched the boundaries of executive power that the British state structure allowed.[16] There are indeed some limits to executive power – perhaps the acquittal of Ponting was such an example of the ability of the British state structure to achieve victory on behalf of the demos against the rulers on some occasions. However, the present British system seems to deliver more scope for abuse than for the protection of rights.

To achieve genuine democratic change in the United Kingdom means to open up political discourses. As long as the same narrow homogeneous band of elites dominate policy-making, ruling on what constitutes threats to the nation's interests without reference to the wider world, and using the legal-rational state to legitimise information control in order to mould political discourse, the state will continue to fail to deliver more democracy to its citizens. Until individuals can voice alternative discourses without fear, not only of arrest and prosecution at the hands of the legal-rational state but also of being ridiculed or dismissed as deviant, unstable, disloyal or subversive by the non-legal-rational tactics the state is equally capable of deploying, democracy will continue to elude us.

There are signs that the traditional dominance of the British political scene by a narrow band of elites with specific ideas about national security will be challenged by the growing assertiveness of other societal groups, the protection of civil liberties afforded by membership in the EU, and the rising democratisation of information sources. The importance of multiculturalism and the assertiveness of groups outside the traditional Old Boys public school/ Oxbridge network might succeed in challenging the establishment that currently governs the UK and sets the parameters of political debate. Changes in communications technology have made access to information more 'democratic' than ever before, and a multiplicity of information sources might mean that the dubious state of a media controlled heavily by monopolistic capitalist interests is challenged. Ready and pluralistic access to international networks of information should, if information is power, serve to empower the citizen. For example, in the realm of national security matters, British researchers have frequently short-circuited the strictly controlled British archives by going to America to use the same documentation, where freedom-of-information policy is more advanced. As the new technologies make information retrieval and exchange ever easier, prospects for more and better research should be enhanced. On the other hand, it might prove to be the case that too much information can be as paralysing as too little, confusing, rather than illuminating, political debate. A multiplicity of 'facts' from different, often competing sources makes the 'truth' hard to acquire. Finally, the security agenda of the European Union is being set without public debate. Secrecy and security policies concentrate power in the hands of EU leaders, with little provision for democratic oversight, transparency or accountability.

Secrecy is more than a series of laws and overt political structures; rather it is something inherent in the prevailing political culture. It has been suggested here that political power flows through complex webs of relationships which alter the intentions and consequences that the state's legal-rational precepts attempt to inscribe. The outputs that emerge are not always those envisaged by policy-makers. There is not necessarily a conspiracy agenda or intention behind the uses and abuses of political power. Nor are they the inevitable outcome of Britain's particular constitutional arrangements. Thus the secret state will not 'wither away' with the wave of a constitutional magic wand. The flow of political power is messy both in theory and in practice, and the task of explaining and reforming the workings of the secret state remains problematic.

NOTES

Chapter 1 Rethinking the British Secret State

1. Graham Greene, 'The virtue of disloyalty', in *The Portable Graham Greene*, ed. Philip Stratford (London: Penguin, 1994), pp 524–7, p. 526.
2. Michel Foucault, 'The juridical apparatus', in W. Connolly (ed.), *Legitimacy and the State* (Oxford: Basil Blackwell, 1984) pp. 201–21, p. 211.
3. Michel Foucault, *Power/Knowledge: selected interviews and other readings*, ed. C. Gordon (Brighton: Harvester, 1980), p. 98.

Chapter 2 The Bureaucratisation of Secrecy

1. Quoted in Gavin Drewry and Tony Butcher, *The Civil Service Today* (Oxford: Basil Blackwell, 1988) p. 175.
2. David Hooper, *Official Secrets: the use and abuse of the Act* (London: Hodder & Stoughton, 1988) p. 26.
3. This account of the origins of the secret state is based on Christopher Andrew, *Secret Service: the making of the British Intelligence Community* (London: Sceptre, 1985) and Philip Knightley, *The Second Oldest Profession: the spy as bureaucrat, patriot, fantasist and whore* (London: Pan, 1986).
4. United Kingdom, Parliament, *Hansard's Parliamentary Debates* (Commons) 5th series 338 (11 July 1889) 85–6.
5. Franks Committee, *Report and Evidence of the Committee on Section 2 of the Official Secrets Act 1911* 4 vols (London: HMSO, 1972) vol. 1, p. 23.
6. A. J. A. Morris, *The Scaremongers: the advocacy of war and rearmament 1896-1914* (London: Routledge & Kegan Paul, 1984) p. 162.
7. Quoted in Nicholas Hiley, 'The failure of British counter-espionage against Germany, 1907–1914', *Historical Journal* 28:4 (1985) pp. 835–62, p. 845; and Morris, *The Scaremongers*, p. 160.
8. Nicholas Hiley, 'Counter-espionage and security during the First World War', *English Historical Review* 101 (July 1986) pp. 635–61, p. 660.
9. Quoted in Andrew, *Secret Service*, p. 54.
10. Knightley, *The Second Oldest Profession*, p. 23.
11. *Hansard* 28 (25 July 1911) 642.
12. *Hansard* 28 (25 July 1911) 643–5.
13. *Hansard* 29 (18 August 1911) 2252.

Chapter 3 Inventing the Enemy, 1919–1945

1. See Andrew Williams, *Trading with the Bolsheviks: the politics of East- -West trade 1920–1939* (Manchester: Manchester University Press, 1992).
2. Arthur Waldron, *The Great Wall of China: from history to myth* (Cambridge: Cambridge University Press, 1990) pp. 182–3.
3. Quoted in Bernard Porter, *Plots and Paranoia: a history of political espionage in Britain 1790–1988* (London: Unwin Hyman, 1989) p. 156.
4. Report from anonymous intelligence agent, 9 January 1919, quoted in Christopher Andrew, *Secret Service: the making of the British Intelligence Community* (London: Sceptre, 1985), p. 335.
5. *The Times* 16 August 1928; 23 August 1928.
6. *The Times* 10 December 1934; 17 December 1934.
7. *The Times* 18 March 1927; 25 March 1927.
8. *The Times* 16 November 1926.
9. *The Times* 12 July 1932; 13 August 1932.
10. *The Times* 18 February 1933.
11. Trial reported in *The Times* between January and March 1938.
12. David Williams, *Not in the Public Interest: the problem of security in democracy* (London: Hutchinson, 1965) p. 89.
13. *The Times* 13 January 1933.
14. Quoted in Williams, *Public Interest,* p. 46.
15. *The Times* 20 April 1939; 20 May 1939.
16. *The Times* 20 November 1935; 28 November 1935.
17. Andrew, *Secret Service,* p. 468.
18. *The Times* 16 May 1927.
19. *The Times* 19 May 1927.
20. *The Times* 22 October 1937; 28 October 1937; Tony Bunyan, *The History and Practice of the Political Police in Britain* (London: Julian Friedmann, 1976) pp. 18–20.
21. See Andrew Lownie, 'Tyler Kent: isolationist or spy?' in Andrew Lownie and Rhodri Jeffreys-Jones, (eds) *North American Spies: New Revisionist Essays* (Edinburgh University Press, 1991) pp. 49–78; Peter Gillman and Leni Gillman, *Collar the Lot: how Britain interned and expelled its wartime refugees* (London: Quartet, 1980), Chap. 12.
22. Lownie, 'Tyler Kent', p. 53.
23. Quoted in Gillman and Gillman, *Collar the Lot,* p. 119.
24. Trial reported in *The Times* 9 August 1940; 20 August 1940; 28 August 1940; 8 November 1940.
25. Quoted in Lownie, 'Tyler Kent', p. 60.
26. Gillman and Gillman, *Collar the Lot,* p. 127.

Chapter 4   The Failure of Cold War Security

1. Quoted in Mark Hollingsworth and Richard Norton-Taylor, *Blacklist: the inside story of political vetting* (London: Hogarth Press, 1988) p. 26.
2. Richard Thurlow, *The Secret State: British internal security in the twentieth century* (Oxford: Blackwell, 1994) p. 280.
3. Quoted in Hollingsworth and Norton-Taylor, *Blacklist*, p. 28.
4. Noel Annan, *Our Age: the generation which made postwar Britain* (London: Fontana, 1991) p. 307.
5. Annan, *Our Age*, p. 308.
6. *The Times* 30 March 1946; 27 May 1948.
7. *The Times* 13 February 1951.
8. *The Times* 2 May 1956.
9. *The Times* 3 July 1952; 10–11 July 1952.
10. Trial reported in *The Times* between 28 January and 29 February 1960.
11. David Hooper, *Official Secrets: the use and abuse of the Act* (London: Hodder & Stoughton, 1988) p. 360.
12. Quoted in Hooper, *Official Secrets*, p. 101–2.
13. Quoted in Hooper, *Official Secrets*, p. 106.
14. Trial reported in *The Times* between 29 April 1963 and 4 September 1963. Also see account in Christopher Andrew and Oleg Gordievsky, *KGB: the inside story of its foreign operations from Lenin to Gorbachev* (London: Hodder & Stoughton, 1990) pp. 429–30.
15. See especially Andrew and Gordievsky, *KGB* pp. 431–5.
16. *The Times* 28 November 1961.
17. Rosamund Thomas, 'The British Official Secrets Act 1911–1939 and the Ponting Case', in Richard Chapman and Michael Hunt (eds) *Open Government* (London: Routledge, 1989) pp. 95–122, pp. 98–9.
18. *The Times* 22 January 1963.
19. See the discussion in Thomas, 'Ponting', p. 97.
20. Trial reported in *The Times* between 9 January 1961 and 18 March 1961. See also Ronald Seth, *Forty Years of Soviet Spying* (London: Cassell, 1965) p. 258; and Fitzroy Maclean, *Take Nine Spies* (London: Weidenfeld & Nicolson, 1978) p. 284, for accounts that later proved false.
21. *Report of the Standing Security Commission* (Cmnd 2722) (London: HMSO, June 1965) p. 19.
22. David Williams, *Not in the Public Interest: the problem of security in democracy* (London: Hutchinson, 1965) , p. 181.
23. *The Times* 23 October 1962.
24. See the Prime Minister's parliamentary address reported in *The Times* 15 November 1962; and also James Margach, *The Abuse of Power: the war between Downing street and the media from Lloyd George to Callaghan* (London: W.H. Allen, 1978) p. 122.

25. Trial reported in *The Times* between 17 March 1965 and 28 May 1965.

26. *The Times* 28 May 1965.

27. Cmnd 2722.

28. *Report of the Security Commission* (Cmnd 3856) (London: HMSO, November 1968) p. 7.

29. *Report of the Security Commission* Cmnd 5362 (London: HMSO, May 1973) pp. 7–8.

30. Bingham's trial reported in *The Times* between 4 April 1972 and 7 June 1972. Maureen Bingham's case reported 13 February 1973.

Chapter 5 Official Secrecy and the Press

1. *Independent on Sunday* 2 September 1990.

2. Patrick Dunleavy and D.B. O'Leary, *Theories of the State* (London: Macmillan, 1987) p. 41.

3. Marjorie Wallace, *Campaign and be Damned: the place of crusading journalism – past and present – in a secretive society* (Second *Guardian* Lecture, 1991) p. 2.

4. *Guardian* 26 October 1990.

5. See the schema proposed by Michael Cockerell, Peter Hennessy and David Walker, *Sources Close to the Prime Minister: inside the hidden world of the news manipulators* (London: Macmillan, 1984) p. 18.

6. Quoted in Cockerell et al., *Sources*, p. 123.

7. Quoted in Cockerell et al., *Sources*, pp. 79–80.

8. Harry Street, 'Secrecy and the citizen's right to know: a British civil libertarian perspective', in Thomas Franck and Edward Weisband (eds) *Secrecy and Foreign Policy* (New York: Oxford University Press, 1974) pp. 332–50, p. 338.

9. David Hooper, *Official Secrets: the use and abuse of the Act* (London: Hodder & Stoughton, 1988), p. 284.

10. *Sunday Express* 8 March 1992, p. 6.

11. *Independent* 6 Feb 1992.

12. Fintan O'Toole, 'You can't put it down', *London Review of Books* (18 July 1996) p. 13.

13. See *Hansard* 135 (2 December 1920) 1537, 1538.

14. *Hansard* 135 (16 December 1920) 966.

15. David Williams, *Not in the Public Interest: the problem of security in democracy* (London: Hutchinson, 1965) p. 27.

16. James Margach, *The Abuse of Power: the war between Downing Street and the media from Lloyd George to Callaghan* (London: W.H. Allen, 1978) pp. 45–7.

17. *The Times* 21 August 1937; *Hansard* 336 (24 May 1938) 1017.
18. Quoted in William Clarke, 'Cabinet secrecy, collective responsibility and the British public's right to know about and participate in foreign-policy making', in Franck and Weisband, *Secrecy*, pp. 202–17, p. 207.
19. Quoted in Hooper, *Official Secrets*, p. 292.
20. *The Times* 8 January 1969.
21. *The Times* 24 January 1969.
22. *The Times* 1 February 1969.
23. Chapman Pincher, *Inside Story: a documentary of the pursuit of power* (London: Sidgwick & Jackson, 1978) p. 177.
24. Quoted in Jonathan Aitken, *Officially Secret* (London: Weidenfeld & Nicholson, 1971) p. 142.
25. Testimony of D-notice Committee secretary Sir Norman Denning, reported in *The Times* 19 January 1971.
26. *The Times* 28 January 1971.
27. *The Times* 25 April 1970.
28. *The Times* 19 June 1976.
29. Quoted in Crispin Aubrey, *Who's Watching You* (Harmondsworth: Penguin, 1981) p. 167.
30. *Peace News* and *The Leveller* were both fined £500, *The Journalist* £200. The fines were later overturned on a technicality by the House of Lords. Hooper, *Official Secrets*, pp. 156–7.
31. *The Times* 20 April 1977.
32. *The Times* 22 April 1978.
33. *The Times* 2 November 1978.
34. *The Times* 18 November 1978.
35. Hooper, *Official Secrets*, p. 155.
36. The best accounts of the Tisdall case are in David Caute, *The Espionage of the Saints: two essays on silence and the state* (Hamish Hamilton, London, 1986) pp. 99–140 and in Hooper, *Official Secrets*, pp. 157–76.
37. *The Times* 14 April 1984.
38. Rosamund Thomas, *Espionage and Secrecy: the Official Secrets Act 1911–1989 of the United Kingdom* (London: Routledge, 1991) pp. 79–80.
39. *The Times* 24 July 1984.
40. *The Times* 26 October 1984.
41. David Northmore, letter to the editor, *Guardian* 31 December 1992.

Chapter 6 Resistence and Reform under Thatcher

1. Richard Thurlow, *The Secret State: British internal security in the twentieth century* (Oxford: Blackwell, 1994) p. 399.
2. Bernard Porter, *Plots and Paranoia: a history of political espionage in Britain 1790–1988* (London: Unwin Hyman, 1989) p. 208.

3. See discussion in Lois McNay, *Foucault: a critical introduction* (Oxford: Blackwell, 1994) pp. 100–2.

4. Quoted in McNay, *Foucault*, p. 102.

5. Quoted in Stephen Dorril, *The Silent Conspiracy: inside the intelligence services in the 1990s* (London: Mandarin, 1994) p. 172.

6. *Security Commission Report* (Cmnd 8540) quoted in Dorril, *Silent Conspiracy*, p. 11.

7. Dorril, *Silent Conspiracy*, p. 139.

8. See the discussion of changing official definitions of subversion in National Council of Civil Liberties, *Report on the Security Service Bill* (pamphlet) (London: NCCL, December 1988).

9. Thurlow, *Secret State*, p. 328

10. Dorril, *Silent Conspiracy*, p. 25–6.

11. Quoted in Dorril, *Silent Conspiracy*, p. 12.

12. The Bettaney case is discussed in Christopher Andrew and Oleg Gordievsky, *KGB: the inside story of its foreign operations from Lenin to Gorbachev* (London: Hodder and Stoughton, 1990) pp. 501–2 and Dorril, *Silent Conspiracy*, pp. 14–35.

13. Porter, *Plots*, p. 220.

14. Dorril, *Silent Conspiracy*, p 16.

15. Dorril, *Silent Conspiracy*, p 24.

16. *The Times* 11 July 1986.

17. Trial reported in *The Times* between 30 November 1982 and 8 December 1982.

18. *The Times* 10 July 1984; 13 July 1984.

19. *The Times* 10 June 1985; 15 June 1985.

20. *The Times* 11 June 1985.

21. *The Times* 29 October 1984.

22. *The Times* 10 January 1986.

23. K.D. Ewing and C.A. Gearty, *Freedom Under Thatcher: civil liberties in modern Britain* (Oxford: Clarendon, 1990) pp. 130–6.

24. David Hooper, *Official Secrets: the use and abuse of the Act* (London: Hodder and Stoughton, 1988), p. 375.

25. Hooper, *Official Secrets*, p. 385.

26. Ewing and Gearty, *Freedom*, pp. 147–52.

27. *Guardian*, 14 October 1988.

28. Hooper, *Official Secrets*, p. 336.

29. *Guardian* 14 October 1988.

30. *Observer* 22 April 1989.

31. *Guardian* 30 Oct 1990.

32. *Guardian* 26 Oct 1990.

33. Dorril, *Silent Conspiracy*, pp. 66–7.

34. David Caute, *The Espionage of the Saints: two essays on silence and the state* (Hamish Hamilton, London, 1986) p. 163.
35. *The Times* 30 November 1982.
36. Hooper, *Official Secrets*, p. 382.
37. Clive Ponting, *The Right to Know: the inside story of the Belgrano Affair* (London: Sphere, 1985) p. 9. In the 1993/4 civil service entrance competition, for 9.4 per cent of the applications, Oxbridge graduates were awarded 40 per cent of the jobs. Oxbridge produces 2 per cent of the yearly national total of graduates. See Walter Ellis, 'The Oxbridge Conspiracy,' *Sunday Times*, 25 September 1994.
38. Ponting, *Right to Know*, p. 8.
39. Ponting, *Right to Know*, p. 139.
40. Ponting, *Right to Know*, p. 139.
41. Richard Norton-Taylor, *The Ponting Affair* (London: Cecil Woolf, 1985) p. 69.
42. Caute, *Espionage*, p. 169.
43. *The Times* 27 April 1940.
44. A similar, but more recent, case is the one in which protestors were charged with causing millions of dollars worth of damage to some fighter planes destined for Indonesia. They were acquitted by a jury on the grounds that their action was to prevent greater wrong – genocide in East Timor.
45. Law Reports Appeals Cases 1964, *Chandler vs DPP* pp. 763–815, p. 764.
46. Rosamund Thomas, 'The British Official Secrets Act 1911–1939 and the Ponting Case', in Richard Chapman and Michael Hunt (eds), *Open Government* (London: Routledge, 1991) pp. 95–122, p. 113.
47. Dorril, *Silent Conspiracy*, p. 58.

Chapter 7 The British State and the Future of Secrecy

1. Tony Bunyan, 'Trevi, Europol and the European state' in Tony Bunyan, ed., *Statewatching the New Europe: a handbook on the European state* (London: Statewatch, 1993) pp. 15–36, p. 33.
2. Stephen Dorril, *The Silent Conspiracy: inside the intelligence services in the 1990s* (London: Mandarin, 1994) p. 244.
3. Quoted in Dorril, *Silent Conspiracy*, p. 248.
4. Quoted in Dorril, *Silent Conspiracy*, p. 252.
5. *Guardian Weekly*, 8 September 1996.
6. K.D. Ewing and C.A. Gearty, *Freedom Under Thatcher: civil liberties in modern Britain* (Oxford: Clarendon, 1990) pp. 164–5.
7. Bernard Porter, *Plots and Paranoia: a history of political espionage in Britain 1790–1988* (London: Unwin Hyman, 1989) p. 208.

8. Tony Bunyan, 'Secret Europe', in *Statewatching*, pp. 37–40, p. 37.

9. Bunyan, 'Secret Europe', p. 37.

10. Bunyan, 'Secret Europe', p. 39.

11. Bunyan, 'Trevi' in Bunyan, *Statewatching*, p. 23.

12. Quoted in Bunyan, 'Trevi', p. 24.

13. Bunyan, 'Trevi', p. 32.

14. Mark Hollingsworth and Richard Norton-Taylor, *Blacklist: the inside story of political vetting* (London: Hogarth Press, 1988) p. 141.

15. Bunyan, 'Trevi', p. 26.

16. Tony Wright, *Citizens and Subjects: an essay on British politics* (London: Routledge, 1994), p. 120.

BIBLIOGRAPHY

Ackroyd, Carol, Margolis, Karen, Rosenhead, Jonathan and Shallice, Tim, *The Technology of Political Control*. 2nd edn. London: Pluto, 1980.

Aitken, Jonathan, *Officially Secret*. London: Weidenfeld & Nicholson, 1971.

Andrew, Christopher, 'The British secret service and Anglo–Soviet relations in the 1920s Part I: from the trade negotiations to the Zinoviev letter', *Historical Journal* 20:3 (1977), pp. 673–706.

Andrew, Christopher, *Secret Service: the making of the British Intelligence Community*. London: Sceptre, 1985.

Andrew, Christopher and Dilks, David (eds), *The Missing Dimension: governments and intelligence services in the twentieth century*. London: Macmillan, 1984.

Andrew, Christopher and Gordievsky, Oleg, *KGB: the inside story of its foreign operations from Lenin to Gorbachev*. London: Hodder & Stoughton, 1990.

Annan, Noel, *Our Age: the generation which made postwar Britain*. London: Fontana, 1991.

Aubrey, Crispin, *Who's Watching You*. Harmondsworth: Penguin, 1981.

Beetham, David, 'Civil liberties, Thatcherism and Charter '88', *Political Quarterly* 60:3 (July 1989) pp. 273–9.

Benn, Tony, *The Right to Know: the case for freedom of information to safeguard our basic liberties*. Nottingham: Institute for Workers' Control, 1978.

Birkenshaw, Patrick, *Freedom of Information: the law, the practice and the ideal*. London: Weidenfeld & Nicholson, 1988.

Bunyan, Tony, *The History and Practice of the Political Police in Britain*. London: Julian Friedmann, 1976.

Bunyan, Tony (ed.), *Statewatching the New Europe: a handbook on the European state*. London: Statewatch, 1993.

Bunyan, Tony, 'Trevi, Europol and the European State', in Bunyan (ed.), *Statewatching*.

Caute, David, *The Espionage of the Saints: two essays on silence and the state*. London: Hamish Hamilton, 1986.

Chapman, Richard and Hunt, Michael (eds), *Open Government*. London: Routledge, 1989.

Clarke, William, 'Cabinet secrecy, collective responsibility and the British public's right to know about and participate in foreign-policy making', in Thomas Franck and Edward Weisband (eds) *Secrecy and foreign policy*. New York: Oxford University Press, 1974.

Cockerell, Michael, *Live from Number 10: the inside story of prime ministers and television*. London: Faber, 1989.

Cockerell, Michael, Hennessey, Peter and Walker, David, *Sources Close to the Prime Minister: inside the hidden world of the news manipulators*. London: Macmillan, 1984.

Cohen, Stanley and Scull, Andrew (eds), *Social Control and the State*. Oxford: Basil Blackwell, 1985.

Connolly, William (ed.), *Legitimacy and the State*. Oxford: Basil Blackwell, 1984.

Costello, John, *Mask of Treachery*. London: Pan, 1989.

Cripps, Yvonne, *The Legal Implications of Disclosure in the Public Interest: an analysis of prohibitions and protection with particular reference to employees and employers*. Oxford: ESC, 1986.

Curran, James, and Seaton, Jean, *Power Without Responsibility: the press and broadcasting in Britain*. 2nd edn. London: Methuen, 1985.

Dandeker, Christopher, *Surveillance, Power and Modernity: bureaucracy and discipline from 1700 to the present day*. Cambridge: Polity Press, 1990.

Delbridge, Rosemary, and Smith, Martin (eds), *Consuming Secrets: how official secrecy affects everyday life in Britain*. London: Bunnett, 1982.

Dorril, Stephen, *The Silent Conspiracy: inside the intelligence services in the 1990s*. London: Mandarin, 1994.

Drewry, Gavin, and Butcher, Tony, *The Civil Service Today*. Oxford: Basil Blackwell, 1988.

Dunleavy, Patrick and O'Leary, D.B., *Theories of the State*. London: Macmillan, 1987.

Ewing, K.D. and Gearty, C.A., *Freedom Under Thatcher: civil liberties in modern Britain*. Oxford: Clarendon, 1990.

Flory, Harriette, 'The Arcos Raid and the rupture of Anglo–Soviet relations, 1927', *Journal of Contemporary History* 12 (1977) pp. 707–23.

Foucault, Michel, *Power/Knowledge: selected interviews and other readings*, ed. C. Gordon. Brighton: Harvester, 1980.

Foucault, Michel, *The Foucault Reader*, ed. Paul Rabinow. London: Penguin, 1984.

Foucault, Michel, 'The juridical apparatus', in W. Connolly, (ed.), *Legitimacy and the state*. Oxford: Basil Blackwell, 1984.

Franck, Thomas and Weisband, Edward (eds) *Secrecy and Foreign policy*. New York: Oxford University Press, 1974.

Freedom of Information Campaign, *Secrecy, or the Right to Know*. London: Library Association, 1980.

French, David, 'Spy Fever in Britain, 1900–1915', *Historical Journal* 21:2 (1978) pp. 355–70.

Gillman, Peter, and Gillman, Leni, *Collar the Lot: how Britain interned and expelled its wartime refugees*. London: Quartet Books, 1980.

Greene, Graham, *The Portable Graham Greene*, ed. Philip Stratford. London: Penguin 1994.

Hanks, Peter and McCamus, John (eds), *National Security: surveillance and accountability in a democratic society*. Cowanswville: Yvon Blais, 1990.

Harrop, Martin (ed.), *Power and Policy in Liberal Democracies*. Cambridge: Cambridge University Press, 1992.

Hazell, Robert, 'Freedom of information in Australia, Canada and New Zealand', *Public Administration* 67 (Summer 1989), pp. 189–210.

Held, David, *Political Theory and the Modern State: essays on state, power and democracy*. Oxford: Basil Blackwell, 1989.

Held, David, *et al.* (eds), *States and Societies*. Oxford: Martin Robertson/Open University, 1983.

Hennessey, Peter, *Whitehall*. London: Fontana, 1989.

Lord Hewart, *The New Despotism*. London: Ernest Benn, 1929.

Hiley, Nicholas, 'The failure of British counter-espionage against Germany, 1907–1914', *Historical Journal* 28:4 (1985) pp. 835–62.

Hiley, Nicholas, 'Counter-espionage and security during the First World War', *English Historical Review* 101 (July 1986) pp. 635–61.

Hollingsworth, Mark and Norton-Taylor, Richard, *Blacklist: the inside story of political vetting*. London: Hogarth Press, 1988.

Hooper, David, *Official Secrets: the use and abuse of the Act*. London: Hodder and Stoughton, 1988.

Jones, Derek and Platt, Steve (eds), *Banned*. London: Channel 4, *New Statesman and Society* and BFI, 1991.

Justice, *Freedom of Expression and the Law*. London: Justice, 1990.

Keane, John, *The Media and Democracy*. Cambridge: Polity Press, 1991.

Kellner, Peter, and Lord Crowther-Hunt, *The Civil Servants: an enquiry into Britain's ruling class*. London: Raven, 1980.

Kernaghan, Kenneth, 'The conscience of the bureaucrat: accomplice or constraint', *Canadian Public Administration* 27:4 (Winter 1984) pp. 576–91.

Knightley, Phillip, *The Second Oldest Profession: the spy as bureaucrat, patriot, fantasist and whore*. London: Pan, 1986.

Leigh, David, *The Frontiers of Secrecy: closed government in Britain*. London: Junction, 1980.

Lichtenberg, Judith (ed.), *Democracy and the Mass Media*. Cambridge: Cambridge University Press, 1990.

Lownie, Andrew, 'Tyler Kent: isolationist or spy?', in Andrew Lownie and Rhodri Jeffreys-Jones (eds) *North American Spies: new revisionist essays*. Edinburgh: Edinburgh University Press, 1991.

Maclean, Fitzroy, *Take Nine Spies*. London: Weidenfeld & Nicolson, 1978.

McNay, Lois, *Foucault: a critical introduction*. Oxford: Blackwell, 1994.

Margach, James, *The Abuse of Power: the war between Downing Street and the media from Lloyd George to Callaghan*. London: W.H. Allen, 1978.

Marsh, Norman (ed.), *Public Access to Government-held Information: a comparative symposium*. London: Stevens & Son, 1987.

Marshall, Geoffrey (ed.), *Ministerial Responsibility*. Oxford: Oxford University Press, 1989.

Martin, David, *Wilderness of Mirrors*. New York: Harper & Row, 1980.

Michael, James, *The Politics of Secrecy: the case for a freedom of information law*. London: National Council for Civil Liberties, 1979.

Minogue, Martin (ed.), *Documents on Contemporary British Government*, vol. 1: *British Government and Constitutional Change*. Cambridge: Cambridge University Press, 1975.

Morris, A.J.A., *The Scaremongers: the advocacy of war and rearmament 1896–1914*. London: Routledge & Kegan Paul, 1984.

National Council of Civil Liberties, *Report on the Security Service Bill* (pamphlet). London: NCCL, December 1988.

Norton-Taylor, Richard, *The Ponting Affair*. London: Cecil Woolf, 1985.

Page, Edward, *Political Authority and Bureaucratic Power: a comparative analysis*. Brighton: Wheatsheaf, 1985.

Pincher, Chapman, *Inside Story: a documentary of the pursuit of power*. London: Sidgwick & Jackson, 1978.

Pincher, Chapman, *Their Trade is Treachery*. London: Sidgwick & Jackson, 1981.

Ponting, Clive, *The Right to Know: the inside story of the Belgrano Affair*. London: Sphere, 1985.

Ponting, Clive, *Whitehall: changing the old guard*. London: Unwin, 1989.

Ponting, Clive, *Secrecy in Britain*. Oxford: Basil Blackwell, 1990.

Porter, Bernard, *Plots and Paranoia: a history of political espionage in Britain 1790–1988*. London: Unwin Hyman, 1989.

Randle, Michael and Pottle, Pat, *The Blake Escape*. London: Sphere, 1989.

Richards, Peter (ed.), *Mackintosh's The Government and Politics of Britain*. 6th edn. London: Hutchinson, 1984.

Right to Know Campaign, *Wouldn't You Like the Right to Know?* London: Right to Know Campaign, December 1992.

Robertson, K.G., *Public Secrets: a study in the development of government secrecy*. London: Macmillan, 1982.

Robertson, K.G., 'Accountable intelligence – the British experience', *Conflict Quarterly* (Winter 1988), pp. 13–28.

Rowat, Donald (ed.), *Administrative Secrecy in Developed Countries*. London: Macmillan, 1979.

Sampson, Anthony, *Anatomy of Britain*. London: Hodder & Stoughton, 1971.

Seth, Ronald, *Forty Years of Soviet Spying*. London: Cassell, 1965.

Seymour-Ure, Colin, *The Political Impact of the Mass Media*. London: Constable, 1974.

Sloman, Anne, and Young, Hugo, *No, Minister: an inquiry into the civil service*. London: BBC, 1982.

Smith, B.C., *Bureaucracy and Political Power*. Sussex: Wheatsheaf, 1988.

Stalker, John, *Stalker*. Harmondsworth: Penguin, 1988.

Street, Harry, 'Secrecy and the citizen's right to know: a British civil libertarian perspective', in Thomas Franck and Edward Weisband (eds) *Secrecy and Foreign Policy*. New York: Oxford University Press, 1974, pp. 332–50.

Thomas, Rosamund, 'The British Official Secrets Act 1911–1939 and the Ponting Case', in Richard Chapman and Michael Hunt (eds) *Open Government*. London: Routledge, 1989, pp. 95–122.

Thomas, Rosamund, *Espionage and Secrecy: the Official Secrets Act 1911–1989 of the United Kingdom*. London: Routledge, 1991.

Thompson, Donald, 'The Committee of 100 and the Official Secrets Act 1911', *Public Law* (1963) pp. 201–26.

Thornton, Peter, *Decade of Decline: civil liberties in the Thatcher years*. London: National Council for Civil Liberties, 1989.

Thurlow, Richard, *The Secret State: British internal security in the twentieth century*. Oxford: Blackwell, 1994.

Tunstall, Jeremy, *The Westminster Lobby Correspondents: a sociological study of national political journalism*. London: Routledge & Kegan Paul, 1970.

Waldron, Arthur, *The Great Wall of China: from history to myth*. Cambridge: Cambridge University Press, 1990.

Wallace, Marjorie, *Campaign and Be Damned! the place of crusading journalism – past and present – in a secretive society*. Second *Guardian* Lecture, 1991.

West, Nigel, *MI5*. London: Triad Grafton, 1983.

West, Nigel, *Molehunt*. London: Coronet, 1987.

West, Rebecca, *The New Meaning of Treason*. New York: Time, 1964.

Whale, John, *The Politics of the Media*. 2nd edn. Glasgow: Fontana/Collins, 1980.

Williams, Andrew, *Trading with the Bolsheviks: the politics of East–West trade 1920–1939*. Manchester: Manchester University Press, 1992.

Williams, David, *Not in the Public Interest: the problem of security in democracy*. London: Hutchinson, 1965.

Wright, Peter, *Spycatcher*. London: Stoddart, 1987.

Wright, Tony, *Citizens and Subjects: an essay on British politics*. London: Routledge, 1994.

Government documents

Franks Committee, *Report and Evidence of the Committee on Section 2 of the Official Secrets Act 1911*, 4 vols. London: HMSO, 1972.

Lord Fulton, *The Civil Service* vol. 1. *Report of the Committee, 1966–68* (Cmnd 3683). London: HMSO, 1968.

Report of the Committee of Privy Counsellors on Cabinet Document Security (Cmnd 6677). London: HMSO, 1977.

Report of the Security Commission (Cmnd 3856) London: HMSO, November 1968.

Report of the Security Commission (Cmnd 5362) London: HMSO, May 1973.

Report of the Security Commission (Cmnd 8876). HMSO: May 1983.

Report of the Standing Security Commission (Cmnd 2722). London: HMSO, June 1965.

United Kingdom, Parliament, *Hansard's Parliamentary Debates* (Commons). London: HMSO.

INDEX